he has had photographs published in the renowned *Birding World*, and is an editor of the *Cork Bird Report*. A member of BirdWatch Ireland, Mark has also contributed to surveys and international projects concerning wildlife and the environment.

This book is dedicated to three people whose lives and inspiration made this guide a reality. To our mother and grandmother Nodlaig Wilson (1922–2012). To Éamon de Buitléar (1930–2013) and Oscar Merne (1943–2013).

The Birds
of Ireland
A FIELD GUIDE

Jim Wilson

Photographs by
Mark Carmody

The Collins Press

First published in 2013 by
The Collins Press
West Link Park
Doughcloyne
Wilton
Cork

A CIP record for this book is available from the British Library.

ISBN: 978-184889-179-1

Design and typesetting by Fairways Design
Typeset in Gill Sans
Plates by Jim Wilson
Printed in Italy by Printer Trento

Contents

Cormorant, Shag, Divers and Grebes — 66

Auks — 75

Seabirds — 81

Tits and Treecreepers — 218

Crows, Starlings and Waxwing — 226

Sparrows, Dunnock, Finches and Buntings — 237

Acknowledgements

As always, I would like to thank Ann, Barry and Peter for putting up with me and being a great help and support and giving me the space and time to write this guide. A very special thanks to Margaret, Carmel, John and Mary for their support in so many ways, especially over the last twelve months.
Jim Wilson

I would like to thank Mary, John, Gillian, Paul, Sandro, Elia and Jasper for having the patience and understanding as I travelled across Ireland taking photographs at weekends instead of visiting them all in Cobh. I hope the book finds good use in your respective homes and beyond!
Mark Carmody

Jim and Mark would like to thank everyone who helped us along the way and the following people for their invaluable support, help and advice in the writing of this book: Alan Lauder, Niall Hatch and all at BirdWatch Ireland, Joey Campbell, Shay Connolly, Aoife Dorney, Des Fay, Joe Hobbs, Niall T. Keogh, Paul Moore, Killian Mullarney, Barry O'Donoghue, Michael John O'Mahony, Glen McArdle, Rónán McLaughlin, Pete Potts and Pat Smiddy.

We would both like to especially thank all at The Collins Press without whom this book would not be possible.

Photo Credits

Mark Carmody took almost all the photos in this guide. We would like to thank the following photographers who helped us to fill the gaps and who generously contributed the following images. These photographers have gone to great lengths to take these photographs and they retain full copyright to those here in this guide and cannot be used elsewhere without prior permission from the photographer: Numbers in brackets after the species name below indicate the image in question, located by counting the images on the plate from left to right and top to bottom. Flock shots are counted as one image. The age/sex of the bird will be included here for clarity if needed.'

Dave Appleton (www.gobirding.eu): Curlew (9 Juv.) p.134; **Robert Bannister** (www.flickr.com/people/75555708@N03/): Hawfinch, p. 253; **Chris Barlow** (www.flickr.com/photos/chrisbarlow75/): Cuckoo (8 Juv.) p. 173; **Tore Berg** (www.flickr.com/photos/28092414@N03/): Velvet Scoter, p. 59, Grey Plover (Juv.) p. 125; **Colum Clarke** (www.southdublinbirds.com): Corncrake (2), p. 119; **Shay Connolly** (www.flickr.com/photos/shayc/):

Starling (middle) p. 5, Blackbird (Leucistic) p. 12, p. 195, Cormorant (7 Ad. Br.) p. 68, Great Northern Diver (2) p. 70, Red-throated Diver (5) p. 71, Red-necked Grebe, p. 74, Gannet (13 diving) p. 84, Water Rail (4) p. 118, Common Sandpiper (6 Juv.) p. 129, Sparrowhawk (12 Juv.), p. 151, Buzzard (7 Juv.) p. 154, Long-eared Owl (2, 3) p. 158, Short-eared Owl (6 on post) p. 159, Skylark (3, 4) p. 190, Black Redstart (2) p. 202, Whitethroat (4, 5) p. 210, Goldfinch (1) p. 241; **Dick Coombes**: Great-spotted Woodpecker (1) p. 177, Lesser Whitethroat p. 215, Bearded Tit (1-4) p. 225; **Dave Curtis** (www.flickr.com/photos/davethebird/): Slavonian Grebe, p. 74, Cattle Egret (NBr.), p. 114, Grey Phalarope (2) p. 143, Sparrowhawk (5 Im.) p. 151, Marsh Harrier (Ad. M.) p. 161, Golden Eagle, p. 163, Stock Dove (4, 6, 7) p. 170, Rock Dove (2) p. 171, Ring Ouzel (3) p. 203, Garden Warbler p. 215, Yellow-browed Warbler p. 217; **Alan Dalton**: Goshawk p. 161; **Dave Dillon** (www.flickr.com/photos/34625967@N04): Ruff (1) p. 140, Nightjar (3) p.174; **Ulf Gotthardsson** (www.flickr.com/photos/ulfgotthardsson/): Lapwing chick, p. 122, Woodcock (4) p. 131; **M. A. Eccles** (www.flickr.com/photos/trampsandhawkers): Goldeneye (Ad. M., Ad. F. main images) p. 55, Pied Flycather (2) p. 127, Red Grouse (5, 8) p. 166, Ring Ouzel (4) p. 203, Crossbill (6 Ad. M.) p. 245; **Cleber C. Ferreira** (www.flickr.com/photos/39052018@N08/): Grey plover (Ad. Br.) p.125; **Steve Greaves** (www.stevegreaves.com): Bittern (4 standing) p. 113, Red Kite (2, 3, 7) p. 155, Buzzard (7 Ad.) p. 154, Quail p. 167; **Floss Gibson** (www.flickr.com/photos/flossgibson/): Sparrowhawk (7 F. perched) p.151, Skylark (Juv.) p. 190; **Mike Grimes** (www.oretani.com): Crane (6, 7, 8) p. 113, Ruff (3) p. 140, Green Sandpiper (3, 4) p. 147, Marsh Harrier (3 Ad. F.) p. 161; **Marlin Harms** (www.flickr.com/photos/28867468@N08/): Red-breasted Merganser (1, 2, 3) p. 56; **Peter Harrison**: Little Auk (1) p. 80, Cory's Shearwater (1, 2) p. 87; **Roger Hatcliffe** (www.flickr.com/photos/lincsbirder/): Teal (Main image of M. in flight) p. 48, Stock Dove (1, 2, 3, 5), p. 170, Fieldfare (2) p. 199, Whinchat (2) p. 203, Yellowhammer (females) p. 250; **Sveinn Jónsson** (www.flickr.com/photos/kjoinn1/): Scaup (M.) p. 61, Long-tailed Duck (M.) p. 61, Little Auk (3) p. 80, Iceland Gull (4) p. 97, Golden Plover (Ad. M. Br.) p. 124, Knot (Ad. Br.) p. 126, Purple Sandpiper (Ad. Br.) p. 139, Merlin (Ad. M and F) p. 153, Long-eared Owl (5, 6, 7) p. 158, White-tailed Eagle (Ad.) p. 163, Rock Dove (1) p. 171, Raven (5, 6) p. 230; **Jordi Jornet** (www.flickr.com/photos/26176588@N04/): Balearic Shearwater (9) p. 87; **Niall T. Keogh**: Jack Snipe, p. 143; **Ross Lennox** (http://www.flickr.com/photos/old_sch00l/): Song Thrush (3) P. 196; **Joe Martin** (www.flickr.com/photos/josh_marvin/): Common Scoter (3 flock) p. 54, Red-breasted Merganser (4) p. 56; **Stephen Mcavoy**: Serin p. 253; **Norman Mackenzie** (www.flickr.com/photos/36678366@N04/): Woodcock (3 Main Image) p. 131, Red Grouse (7 F.) p. 166; **Rónán Mclaughlin** (www.flickr.com/people/ronanmclaughlin/): Blackcap p.13, Corncrake p. 24, (1, 3) p. 119, Gadwall (2) p. 47, Garganey (M.) p. 59, Sandwich Tern (2) p. 99, Pomarine Skua, p. 107, Snowy Owl (1) p. 161, Fieldfare (4) p. 199, Black Redstart (1) p. 202, Pied Flycatcher (1) p. 217; **Richard T. Mills**: Shelduck (ducklings) p. 44, Common Scoter (bottom right M.), p. 54, Black-necked Grebe (Moulting) p. 74, Black Tern (3, 4) p. 107, Woodcock (5) p. 131, Nightjar (2) p. 174, Firecrest, p. 217; **Allan Morgan**: Green-winged Teal, p. 59, Long-tailed Skua, p. 107, Pectoral Sandpiper (6) p. 145; **Joaquim Muchaxo** (www.flickr.com/photos/jmuchaxo/): Balearic

Shearwater (10) p. 87; **Killian Mullarney**: Great Black-backed Gull (1, 9, 10) p. 90, Lesser Black-backed Gull (4, 5, 7, 8) p. 91, Lapwing (6 Ad. NBr.) p. 122, Dunlin (Ad. NBr.) p. 127; **Barry O'donoghue** (www.henharrierireland. blogspot.ie/): Hen Harrier (4) p. 156; **Michael John O'mahony** (www.flickr. com/photos/griangraf/): Grey Phalarope (1) p. 143, Wood Sandpiper (1) p. 147, Kestrel (10 Ad. M) p. 150, Sparrowhawk (11) p. 151, Peregrine (6) p. 152, Merlin (7) p. 153, Buzzard (1, 9) p. 154, Hen Harrier (3) p. 156, Short-eared Owl (3, 7, 8), p. 159, Red Grouse (1, 2) p. 166, Cuckoo (5) p. 173, Sand Martin (1, 3) p. 180, House Martin (1) p. 181; **John N. Murphy** (http://murfswildlife.blogspot.ie/): Barnacle Goose (5 standing) p. 42, Bean Goose p. 59, Great Northern Diver (7 Ad. NBr.) p. 70, Spoonbill (2) p. 113, Red Grouse (6, 9) p. 166, Whitethroat (1, 2) p. 210, Crossbill (Juv.) p. 245; **Reynir Skarsgård** (www.flickr.com/photos/32203824@N00/): Greylag Goose (main flight image) p. 41, Arctic Tern (Juvs.) p. 101, Redwing (1) p. 198; **Silvio Sola** (www.flickr.com/photos/81499140@N03/): Brambling (1) p. 243; **Matti Suopajärvi** (www.flickr.com/people/mattisj/): Grey Plover (5 in flight) p. 125, Woodcock (flight shots) p. 131; **Jerry Ting** (www.flickr. com/photos/jerryting/): Ruff (2) p. 140; **Jeremiah Trimble** (www.flickr.com/ photos/7487520@N08/): Leach's Petrel p. 87; **Bob Weaver**: Crossbill (1, 2, 3, 4, 6, 7) p. 245; **Jim Wilson** (www.irishwildlife.net): Barnacle Goose (7, 8) p. 42, Shelduck (Juv.) p. 44, Eider (1, 2, 4, 5, 7, 8, 9, 10, 11, 12) p. 53, Red-breasted Merganser (5, 6, 7) p. 56, Cormorant (8, 10) p. 68, Shag (5) p. 69, Great Northern Diver (1, 4, 8) p. 70, Guillemot with Razorbill (6) p. 76, Puffin (1, 7) p. 78, Black Guillemot (8) p. 79, Manx Shearwater (3 flock) p. 82, Gannet (1, 6, 11, 15, 16) p. 84, Fulmar (4, 5, 6) p. 85, Great Shearwater (3, 4) p. 85, Glaucous Gull (6) p. 96, Kittiwake (2, 9) p. 98, Arctic Tern (6, 7) p. 101, Arctic Skua (3, 4, 7, 9, 10) p. 102, Great Skua (10) p. 103, Kestrel (6) p. 150, Peregrine (9, 11) p. 152, Buzzard (5, 6, 10) p. 154, Long-eared Owl (1) p. 158, Pheasant (1, 2, 7) p. 165, Woodpigeon (1, 2, 4, 5, 6, 7, 10) p. 169, Feral Pigeon (7) p. 171, House Martin (4, 5, 8) p. 181, Swallow (9) p. 182, Pied Wagtail (1) p. 186, Robin (4) p. 194, Song Thrush (2, 4, 7) p. 196, Mistle Thrush (3) p. 197, Wheatear (3, 8) p. 201, Blackcap (6) p. 208, Great Tit (1) p. 221, Jackdaw (2, 7) p. 228, Rook (4) p. 229, Hooded Crow (7, 9) p. 231, Magpie (1, 5, 7, 9) p. 233, Rose-coloured Starling (Juv.) p. 236, House Sparrow (3, 7, 10), p. 238, Chaffinch (3) p. 242, Bullfinch (Juv.) p. 244, Greenfinch (7, 8) p. 246; **Peter Wilson** (www.flickr.com/photos/foilistpeter/): Pied Wagtail (7) p. 186, Long-tailed Tit (1) p. 223; **Nigel Winnu** (www.flickr.com/ photos/winnu/): Snowy Owl (2) p. 161; **Ron Wolf** (www.flickr.com/photos/ rwolf/): Black-throated Diver p. 74; **Peter William Wort** (www.flickr.com/ photos/28878705@N08/): Great Spotted Woodpecker (6) p. 177.

A male Chaffinch

Introduction

To some, birdwatching might, on the surface, look like a strange pastime involving a few people dressed in camouflage jackets running around the countryside looking for some small brown birds. But birdwatching is a lot more than that. We are all birdwatchers to a greater or lesser degree. At some stage or other each of us has had our attention drawn to a wild bird, whether looking at a cheeky Robin in the garden, watching seagulls during a day at the beach in summer or when feeding the swans at the local pond.

Birdwatching can become a lifetime hobby. Its beauty is that birds are everywhere, from the windowsill in the centre of a town or city to the cliff tops of the most remote, windswept island. So you can birdwatch anywhere, any time, and anyone can do it, no matter what their age, sex or physical ability. Even if you are confined to home, to bed, or to a wheelchair, you are in business as long as you have even the most limited window to the outside world. Once you are bitten by the bug (or bird!), there is no limit to the level of enjoyment and knowledge to be gained from studying even one bird species. Whole books, for instance, have been written about the Robin alone. Through birdwatching you can also get involved in practical conservation work by taking part in national and international surveys. You can make a valuable contribution to our knowledge and the conservation of birds.

Birdwatching is also one of the best introductions, both for young and old, to the natural world around us. You may find that your attention will be drawn to the flowers and plants which birds use, or to the multitude of creatures, big and small, on which they prey. Most good birdwatchers are also very knowledgeable about plants, animals, butterflies and moths, and even weather forecasting. Many of the most famous naturalists began as birdwatchers.

Note: In recent years the terms 'birding' instead of 'birdwatching' and 'birder' instead of 'birdwatcher' have become popular amongst many experienced birdwatchers in Ireland. The authors prefer the terms 'birdwatching' and 'birdwatcher' and these will be used throughout this guide.

Identifying Ireland's Birds

Getting Started

Bird identification is basically an exercise in observation. It makes you examine more closely everything you see and hear. With practice you will learn to gather a lot of information in a short space of time about the birds you find. Sometimes it can be very easy, as some birds such as the Magpie have very obvious features that are unique to them. Other times, for the differentiation of birds that look very similar, such as the Willow Warbler and Chiffchaff, it is a bit like those 'spot the difference' puzzles where two images are presented that look identical but have very subtle differences, and you have to look carefully to see them. Even if you can identify only a dozen different birds, by looking at them and memorising what they look like, you will notice that there is something different about any 'new' bird which appears. The topics discussed in this chapter will help you on your way to becoming a confident birdwatcher with the ability to identify birds you see and help you get more enjoyment from your hobby.

A Willow Warbler and a Chiffchaff – a difficult identification challenge.

The Notebook

Apart from this guide, the most important book you will need when birdwatching is your notebook. This is used to write down what, where and when you have seen and heard, and anything you feel is important to keep as a record. It should also be used to take descriptions of birds you cannot readily identify. Without your notebook, by the time you get out this guide the bird may well have flown away, never to be seen again. You won't be able to remember complicated plumage details, blue may become green, grey may turn to black, streaking disappears, and size and shape become distorted. You may end up convincing yourself that the bird you spotted is the same as the first bird you come across in the book which looks vaguely like it, passing over 'minor' details such as its extreme rarity or the fact that there are other very similar species which are far more common than the one you have picked out. Making a quick sketch of any mystery bird you see is also very valuable. With a little practice, you can record a large amount of information about a bird in this way in a short space of time. You do not need a degree in art. In fact, you do not need to be able to draw well at all. If you think about it, if you wanted to give someone directions you would probably draw a map rather than have them remember the directions in their head. When identifying birds it is the same thing – think of your humble sketch as a map rather than a work of art. You can practise your observation skills by describing and sketching birds you know that are easy to find and watch, such as birds in your garden or at a local pond or woodland. Then compare your notes with the species images and text in this guide and see how well you observed the birds. Taking notes makes you to look more closely and systematically at the birds you see and hear, and helps you become a better birdwatcher. *Note*: most mobile phones have a sound record option and this could also be used to record your bird description. If the bird is making any sounds, these can sometimes be loud enough to record also.

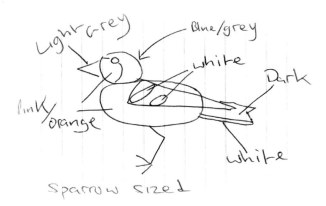

Chaffinch – a basic sketch can capture a lot of information quickly.

Plumage and 'Bare Parts' Terminology

In order to make accurate descriptions of the birds you see, you should get to know the names of the different parts of a bird. Feathers on almost all birds are arranged in groups called feather tracts. These tracts are common to most birds and can vary between species in the number and/or shape of the feathers in each tract. The labelled photographs below show the names of the various parts and tracts of a bird. Look at the photos and labels and try to become familiar with the various names. This will help you when confronted with a bird that you have never seen before and need to describe accurately in order to identify it. Use the species photos in this guide to practise naming the different parts, and don't worry if you can't remember them all: you will get to know them with time.

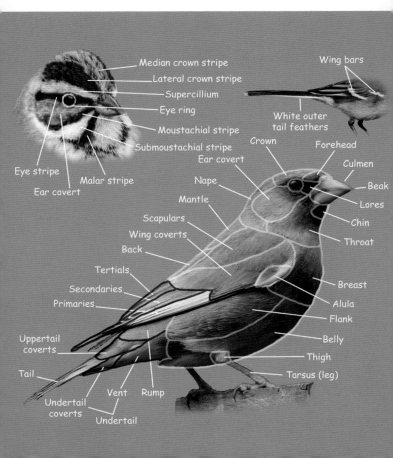

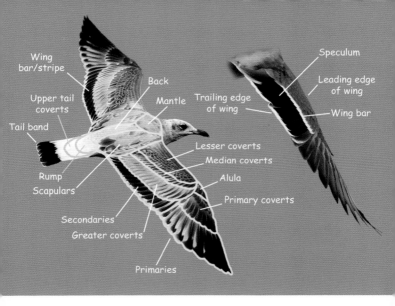

Wing bar/stripe

Back

Upper tail coverts

Mantle

Tail band

Rump

Scapulars

Secondaries

Greater coverts

Primaries

Lesser coverts

Median coverts

Alula

Primary coverts

Speculum

Leading edge of wing

Trailing edge of wing

Wing bar

Moult in Birds

Bird identification would be very easy if each bird species had the same plumage colour and pattern all the time. What can make birdwatching a challenge for even the most experienced birdwatcher is feather moult, that process by which birds change plumage from juvenile to adult, from breeding to non-breeding and all stages in between. A very important part of bird identification is being aware of and understanding the basics of feather moult.

Feathers must be strong, light and flexible to do their work. Without them, birds cannot fly or stay warm. Like mammals

For some birds, like the Starling, moult can make the same bird look different at various times of the year.

shedding old hairs as new ones grow, birds replace old feathers with new ones regularly. However, unlike humans, who shed hair continuously, birds generally replace their feathers only at certain times of the year. Birds have also evolved a system of replacing or moulting feathers in sequence to ensure that feather function is maintained. The main flight feathers, the primaries and secondaries, are usually replaced in a predictable sequence, starting with the innermost primary and continuing outward from the body, while the outermost secondary is first replaced, continuing inward towards the body. The new feathers grow in place of the old ones, pushing them out. This results in gaps where the old feathers have dropped off and the new ones are not yet fully grown, most evident on the wings and tail. Most land birds moult in such a way that they are always able to fly. Crows in late June and July have their wings and tails in moult, with some individuals flying around almost tailless and with many wing feathers missing but still enough to stay airborne. Ducks, swans and geese moult all of their flight feathers at the same time and as a result are flightless for four to six weeks.

Unfortunately, there is no 'one-size-fits-all' moult pattern for birds. The pattern of moult varies between individuals and species, though thankfully different bird groups, such as gulls, ducks and finches, typically follow predictable moult patterns. For most birds, moult takes place outside the breeding and migration periods. Most adult birds seen in Ireland moult all their feathers each year after breeding. Bigger birds, such as the gulls, moult body feathers a second time in the spring, and recently fledged young birds will usually replace their body feathers and some wing feathers in their first autumn, subsequently having a complete annual moult at that time. There are exceptions, such as the young of House Sparrows and Starlings, which undergo a full moult of all their feathers in their first autumn. Most birds have a recognisable juvenile plumage which is usually replaced shortly after fledging. Small birds reach adult plumage within a year or two of hatching, while bigger birds can take longer. Large gulls, such as the Herring Gull, take three years of plumage changes to reach adult plumage. Eagles are in almost continuous moult and take up to six years to reach adult plumage.

The timing of moult can be different for males and females. Like most Irish duck species, the male Mallard, for example, moults in June and does it so fast it is flightless for up to four weeks, while the female moults and becomes flightless only after the young are independent, typically in July or August. For the Mute Swan it is the exact opposite: the female becomes flightless two or three weeks after the cygnets have hatched while the male starts moulting only when the female regains her full power of flight. Some of our migratory birds moult completely before leaving Ireland; others have a partial moult here, pause it during migration and finish the process on arrival at their summer or wintering grounds, while a few will wait until the migration flight is over.

Trauma and shock can cause a bird to lose some of its feathers, which are usually replaced straight away, and disease and starvation can cause a bird to suspend its moult until it recovers or finds a food supply.

All these moult-related plumage changes can result in the same bird species looking different at different times of the year and at different ages before adulthood.

Don't worry if you find moult complicated and confusing. As you watch the birds around you more and more, you will notice patterns emerging, such as Black-headed Gulls losing their dark hood in winter and Black-tailed Godwits gaining their rusty breeding plumage in spring. You will eventually get to know the moulting patterns of different species which will help you identify some birds and get a greater understanding of the lives of others.

Moult in waders and gulls

Some waders and gulls when not in adult plumage are considered to be among the most challenging in bird identification, so understanding their annual moult patterns will help to identifiy them.

All young waders and gulls start out with juvenile plumage which they usually keep until they arrive at their wintering grounds. There they have a 'post-juvenile moult', also called a partial moult, replacing all the body feathers and some of the inner wing coverts with new feathers that have different colours and patterns from the juvenile plumage. All waders have a partial moult, usually sometime

Juv.

Juv. during moult to 1st. W.

1st W.

Dunlin

In autumn young waders moult from juvenile to first winter plumage, presenting an identification challenge.

October → June → October

new wing coverts

1st S.

Juv/1st W.

2nd W.

new tail & body feathers

Mediterranean Gull

new primaries

old primaries

Moult in gulls can take up to six weeks; they can undergo up to four years of plumage change to reach adult plumage.

between January and April, so it is sometimes referred to as a 'spring moult', and then a complete moult, later in the year, usually sometime between August and November. Most waders reach adult plumage within 12 months of hatching. Gulls, on the other hand, take longer. Small gulls, such as the Black-headed Gull, take just over a year, medium-sized gulls, such as the Common Gull, take a little over two years, while big gulls, such as Herring Gull, take a little over three years.

Because moulting takes a few weeks and varies from individual to individual, you might encounter birds with mostly old feathers, a mixture of old and new, or mostly new feathers, all standing side by side.

Feather wear

While some species use feather moult to change into breeding plumage, others such as sparrows, buntings and chats rely on feather wear to turn their dull non-breeding plumage into attractive breeding plumage. When feathers are exposed to the sun's UV rays for long periods they become brittle. Pale feather areas, such as edges or tips, become brittle more quickly than dark parts of the feathers. In winter, male House Sparrows have a very small indistinct black bib, but by the time the breeding season comes around it is a large black bib. They get this because the new breast feathers they grew the previous autumn were black with pale tips, and over time these pale tips became brittle and fell off, leaving the dark part of the feathers to form the black bib. Starlings do a similar thing, having pale tips to their dark feathers in winter, which

A male House Sparrow in breeding plumage gets its large black bib through the wearing-off of the pale tips of dark feathers at the end of winter.

make them look spotted, but which then wear off leaving an almost all-dark, glossy breeding plumage, without the need for a moult.

What to Look for When Identifying a Bird

Sometimes we only get a few seconds or minutes to look at a bird before it flies away or dives into a bush, never to be seen again. Obviously, the more details you can get the easier it will be to identify the bird, and the key pieces of information you need to focus on are: Size, Shape, Patterns, Colours, Sounds, Habits and Movement, 'Jizz', Habitat and Time of Year observed. If possible, record as much of this information as you can before you look at the species descriptions in this guide.

The Dunlin and Turnstone furthest away from the lens look bigger than those closer up. The bird on the right is a Ruff.

Size

Birds are rarely found on their own: there are nearly always other birds close by. If there is a bird you know nearby, compare its size with your mystery bird and note down any differences, e.g. smaller than a Robin or the same size as a Woodpigeon. Try to do this without looking through binoculars or a telescope as these can create an optical illusion which makes things which are further away look bigger. Light conditions can also affect your impression of size: a pale bird against a pale background will look bigger than the same bird against a dark background. The reverse is true for dark birds. A bird might fluff up its feathers, making it look bigger than usual, or flatten them, making the same bird look unusually small.

Tail shapes: forked, notched, square, rounded, wedge.

Shape

When identifying a bird, judging its shape is very important. The essential parts of a bird to look at in relation to this are the beak, legs, wings and tail. Is the beak thin like a blue tit's, or thick like a Greenfinch's? Are the legs short or long, thin or fat? Are the wings long and narrow like a swift or broad and short like a Pheasant's? Is the tail relatively long like a Magpie's or short like a Blue Tit's? It

With practice birds can be identified even in silhouette.

The shape of a beak can help identify a bird.

is also very useful to note the shape of the end of a bird's tail – is it square, rounded, wedged, notched or forked? As with judging size, a bird's shape can vary dramatically depending on whether its feathers are raised or flat against the body. Moult can also make long-tailed birds look short-tailed.

Patterns

The variety of patterns, stripes, lines, patches, bars, spots, etc., on birds is almost infinite. Recording the most striking patterns is important. Firstly, note any wing patterns. Are there any patches or wing bars or wing stripes? Then check the tail: is it all one colour? Look carefully: many birds, such as wagtails and buntings, have pale outer tail feathers which are not always easy to see. Are there light or dark bars on the tail? The tails of young gulls might have a dark terminal tail band (on the end). The bird's back might be plain or striped, sometimes very subtly, but even subtle patterns can sometimes help identify a bird. The underside of the body might be plain, streaked, spotted, or a combination of all three! Head patterns on birds can be very complex. The Blackbird has a plain head pattern but the Blue Tit has a very complex one. Be aware

Feather patterns on birds can vary from plain or subtle like a Blackbird (left) to very complicated like a Blue Tit (right).

that feather moult can also affect the size and shape of plumage patterns. Record any features that stand out and, as mentioned already, try to get to know the different parts of a bird by studying them on pp. 4–5. Don't worry if you can remember only some of the parts. Your knowledge will improve with practice.

Light conditions can play tricks on the observer, making plumage look lighter, darker or even a different colour.

Colours

One area of bird identification that can cause great difficulty is describing in words the colours of birds. For instance, Rooks are not actually black but a beautiful dark iridescent blue. Light conditions and wear of the feathers affect colour, as will whether the

A leucisitc Blackbird: the white feathers are a result of no colour pigment being produced for them, usually the result of a genetic anomaly but can also be caused by shock.

feathers are wet or dry. Try to refer to the colours of birds you already know: for example 'Robin' red, 'Blue Tit' blue, etc. It is not always enough to say that a bird was brown, and you should try to be more exact. For instance, it might be greyish brown, i.e. mainly brown with a hint of grey, or reddish brown, which is also mainly brown but with a hint of red. Both of these colours are basically brown, but look completely different from each other. Some birds can be leucistic or albino, conditions which result in parts or all of the bird's feathers being washed-out looking or white. This is most noticeable on birds with dark plumage. Also, as feathers get old their colour can fade or change. These plumage variations might make it hard to identify a bird that would otherwise be easy to identify. Finally, remember to record the colour of the bird's bare parts: legs, beak, eyes and any surrounding bare skin. Beware – wet or dry mud or earth on beak and legs will often hide the real colour.

Sounds

Birds make lots of different sounds, some of which are so distinctive that you can identify some birds without seeing them. Bird calls and songs have been the inspiration for many poets, such as Shakespeare, Hardy and Clarke, and composers such as Mahler, Sibelius, Ravel, and many traditional Irish musicians. But try as they may, even these experts in sound have struggled to replicate accurately what birds really sound like. What is the difference between a call and a song? A call is typically very short and not at all musical. There are

The 'song' of a bird like this Blackcap can seem beautiful to our ears but to other birds can be a strong message to stay away.

two main types of bird call: the contact call and the alarm call. An example of the contact call is the calls of finches in a flock as they fly over a field, or that of a flock of Long-tailed Tits moving along a hedgerow. These contact calls help keep the flock together. The other type of call is the alarm call, usually louder than a contact call and often used to raise the alarm when danger is near. The song, on the other hand, is usually very musical to our ears, and is used primarily to attract a mate and tell rival birds of its own kind to keep out of its territory.

If you do not have a sound recorder or your mobile phone handy to record the song or call of your mystery bird, then write down what it sounded like to you. Drawing a song 'graph' might help, to show where the notes went up or down, relative to each other, and where and for how long there were pauses between notes. People have used words and phrases to remind them of the sound or structure of a bird's song. For example, a Yellowhammer 'says' something like 'a little bit of bread and no cheese'. Separating the calls of the Collared Dove and Woodpigeon is easy if you remember that Collared Doves seem to say, *'Can yoouuu coo ... can yoouuu coo ...'*, while the similar-sounding Woodpigeon says, *'take two, John, take two'*. There are some very reliable websites with excellent libraries of bird sounds, such as www.xeno-canto.org.

Habits and Movement

It is also important to note what the bird is doing. Is it wagging its tail all the time? Is its stance upright or almost horizontal? Is it always on the ground or in bushes? Is its flight fast and straight like a wren or undulating like a finch? Does it fly close to the ground or high in the air? Does it stay out in the open or hide deep in a bush most of the time? Is it calling continuously? Is it singing out in

The Wren has a habit of cocking its tail in the air, something that can help identify the bird with seeing any plumage details.

the open or out of sight? Recording this information can be very important when identifying a bird.

Jizz

'Jizz' is a term used by birdwatchers to describe that almost indescribable element of a bird's appearance. It usually becomes recognisable when you get familiar with a species. For example, you would be able to identify a good friend even if they were quite far away, with a completely new hairstyle and clothes, because of the combination of the way they walk, hold themselves, their size, body proportions, etc., which, when taken all together, are unique to that person. It is the same for birds.

Habitat

Where you see your mystery bird can be very important. Make a note of what the general habitat is, i.e. wetland, garden, forest, etc. While birds do turn up away from their preferred habitats, most will seek them out.

Time of Year

The time of year you see a bird can also be important. Many of the birds we see in Ireland are migrants, either coming here to breed, such as the Swallow, for the winter, such as the Whooper Swan, or just passing through on migration, such as the Whimbrel. While it is always possible to see a particular species at almost any time of the year, most are found at certain times of the year and seeing one outside their usual time should make you cautious about its identification. Also, during migration, birds that are scarce or rare in Ireland can get blown off course and end up here. For instance, American waders can get caught up in autumn storms while migrating from Arctic North America to their wintering grounds in Central and South America, and so are more likely to be seen here at that time of year.

Binoculars and Telescopes

Binoculars, telescopes and cameras are some of the important tools a birdwatcher uses when identifying and studying birds. Like cars, they range from the very cheap and nasty, via the practical and reliable 'value for money' models, right up to incredibly expensive equipment which sometimes functions mainly as a status symbol. If you do your homework before choosing, you can get a pair of binoculars and/or a telescope that will last you a lifetime, for less than the price of a weekend away.

Porro prism binoculars (left) and roof prism binoculars (right).
(Courtesy Opticron)

Binoculars

When it comes to birdwatching, a pair of binoculars should definitely be the next purchase after your identification guide and notebook. Birds have an unfortunate habit of flying away if you get too close. This can be thought of as part of the challenge, or sometimes the frustration, of birdwatching. The more interested you become in birds and their identification the more apparent it will be that, to learn more about them, you will need to get a closer look, and binoculars are essential to do this without disturbing them. You may be dazzled and sometimes confused by the array of binoculars available and the jargon used to describe them. Understanding how binoculars work will help you choose a pair that is right for you.

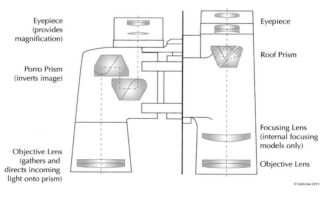

The inside of the two main types of binoculars. (Courtesy Opticron).

There are two basic types of binoculars on the market: the old-style porro prism binoculars and the newer roof prism binoculars. The porro prism binoculars can be very good but need to be handled with care as they can be easily damaged by even a light bang and are rarely totally waterproof. Roof prism binoculars, which look like two tubes, are very streamlined and are usually very comfortable to hold. Compact binoculars, while being small enough to fit into your hand, have small objective lenses and so do not let in much light and have a small field of view. They can be handy if you are travelling abroad and want to keep your baggage weight down, or if you just don't want to carry a bigger/heavier pair of binoculars around with you.

When getting your first pair of binoculars, start with something that is not too expensive because, until you get used to handling them, you are at a greater risk of dropping or damaging them. You can spend anything from €80 to €1,800 on standard binoculars. Usually very cheap binoculars are easily broken and have poor-quality lenses that will have you seeing double after a while. You should be able to get a good pair to begin with from about €150–€200. If you become more interested in birdwatching and find yourself using the binoculars a lot, you can then upgrade.

Look for a combination of two numbers near the eyepieces on binoculars, e.g. 10x50. These will tell you most of the information you need before making a purchase. The first number refers to the magnification of the image made by the binoculars, i.e. 10x means ten times the actual size of the image. The second number refers to the diameter in millimetres of the lenses furthest from your eyes when looking through them, which are called objective lenses. The bigger this number, the more light gets through to your eyes, and so the brighter the image. For general use 7x30, 8x30 or 8x40 binoculars are ideal: fairly powerful but light and compact. Don't go for the biggest, most powerful binoculars as they can be very heavy, so they will be difficult to keep steady and will be tiring to hold up for more than a few minutes. If you wear glasses make sure the binoculars have what is called good eye relief. This is the distance from the surface of the eyepiece to the observer's eye that allows the observer to see the complete field of view. The longer the eye relief the better, allowing an observer with glasses to use binoculars without having to remove their glasses.

Always remember that having the most up-to-date equipment will not automatically make you a better birdwatcher. In camera shops that sell second-hand equipment, good cheap binoculars can sometimes be found, but if at all possible only buy a pair of binoculars after looking through them first. People have individual tastes and requirements, and different makes and designs will suit different people. After all, if the binoculars are not comfortable for you and your eyes, they will probably not be used very often or, worse, may end up damaging your eyesight over time. If you are not in a position to go to a shop to buy a pair, all the binoculars in the BirdWatch Ireland shop (www.birdwatchireland.ie) are selected to suit most budgets and have been tested by birdwatchers.

Adjusting binoculars before use

Adjusting binoculars before using them is vital. All binoculars are basically two monoculars, called barrels, which are connected by a central column and focusing wheel. The distance between the barrels is adjustable because the distance between our eyes varies from person to person. Adjust the distance while looking through them by using a bending action on the binoculars barrels until you see one circular image. This is the correct barrel distance for you. Eyesight varies from person to person and often one eye is better than the other. To adjust your binoculars for this, put a piece of paper or thin cardboard over the barrel with the adjustable eyepiece and, using the central focusing wheel, focus on something with sharp contrast about 15 or 20 metres away, such as a signpost or poster. Then block the barrel with the fixed eyepiece and focus on the same signpost or poster with the adjustable eyepiece until the image is sharp. The binoculars are now adjusted to suit your eyes. When setting up and adjusting your binoculars do not block your eye with your hand because the pressure of the hand on the closed eye can temporarily impair vision in that eye and so defeat the purpose of the exercise. Often there are numbers on the side of the adjustable eyepiece, so you can remember the setting that suits you. If you cannot afford to buy a pair of binoculars, someone might have a broken pair and if the side with the adjustable eyepiece is undamaged it could be used as a monocular.

Remember the following tips when choosing binoculars:

1. Don't be tempted to buy the first pair of binoculars you look at. You will be hoping to get long use from them and it is wise to shop around.

2. Before looking through the binoculars, check for scratches on the glass or bumps on the surface and make sure that the central focusing wheel moves freely.

3. Look through the opposite end of the binoculars for damage or dust inside. (This applies to telescopes also.)

4. There should be a coating on the lenses, usually blue but sometimes green or yellow.

5. Adjust the focusing as explained above.

6. Be sure there is no noticeable colour difference between the objects you are looking at with the naked eye and what you see through the binoculars.

7. Some binoculars can focus on closer objects than others. The closer to you they can focus the better.

8. Check for the amount of blurring (if any) at the edges of the image in view; the less the better.

9. The weight of the binoculars is very important. As already mentioned, holding binoculars up to your eyes for even a few minutes can be quite tiring. Make sure you are comfortable with them.

Practise with your new binoculars as often as possible. Look at objects at different distances and heights and try to find and focus on them as quickly as possible. Many people find locating a bird with binoculars quite difficult at first but with just a little practice it will become second nature. The secret is to fix your eyes on the bird or object and then, without looking away from it, place the binoculars to your eyes. Being able to grip and raise your binoculars to your eyes without taking them off the bird is very important.

The strap on your binoculars should be adjusted so they do not bounce all over the place when you are walking. The best position is at or about chest level, and make sure you can take them off easily without getting the strap caught around your head. Just like the gunslingers in the Wild West, you need to be quick off the draw with your binoculars to get a close look at a bird that might not wait around for long.

Telescopes

Binoculars are great for most birdwatching situations, especially in woodlands and where birds are moving about quickly. However, if you want to watch birds at sea or on an estuary or lake, where they usually do not move too fast, are easy to locate and can often be quite a distance away, a telescope is especially useful. There are two main types of telescope: the traditional 'straight through' telescope and one with an angled eyepiece.

Both are good, but a telescope with an angled eyepiece is generally more comfortable to use and great if rested on a low wall or rock. A telescope suitable for birdwatching will cost you over €200, with some over €1,000. Do not buy an astronomical telescope, which is specifically for looking at the stars (usually white or red in colour). These are generally too powerful and awkward

A telescope with an angled eyepiece, a popular choice amongst birdwatchers. (Courtesy Opticron)

to use and if they are cheap will often have poor quality glass and break easily. A good birdwatching telescope should have a magnification of between 20x and 30x and an objective lens of at least 60mm and, as with binoculars, should above all suit you. Many telescopes now come with a selection of eyepieces, often sold separately from the body, which allows you to choose one that suits you and your budget. For some models you can get a zoom eyepiece which can be handy as you can scan for birds at a low magnification and then zoom in for a closer look at an individual. When it comes to telescopes and other optical equipment, you get what you pay for, and while a good zoom eyepiece can be expensive, it should be worth it in the long run.

BirdWatch Ireland's shop (www.birdwatchireland.ie) stocks a large range of binoculars, telescopes and accessories to suit all pockets and its staff can offer expert advice. All profit from sales is used to help bird conservation in Ireland.

Care for Binoculars and Telescopes

Your binoculars will usually come with a case, but if you want to use them for birdwatching you will have to leave the case at home, or in your bag or car. This is because you always have to be ready for that split-second chance of seeing something new or unusual, and by the time you get the binoculars out of the case the bird is gone. Your binoculars and telescope will be regularly exposed to the elements and, therefore, it is very important to remember a few simple tips to increase the lifespan of your prized possessions.

1. Buy or make a rain/dust-guard which will cover both eyepieces of your binoculars at the same time and which can be attached to the strap.

2. Before attempting to clean the glass on binoculars or other optical equipment, first remove grit or sand from inside the rims with a dry artist's paintbrush or camera airbrush. Grit and sand will scratch the glass during cleaning.

3. Use only a clean, dry, soft cloth to clean the lenses on binoculars, telescopes and cameras. Tissues leave fibres on the glass and will eventually damage it.

4. Do not rub the lenses too hard as this will eventually remove the special optical coating; be very gentle.

5. If you get seawater on your optical equipment, wipe it down with a warm, slightly damp cloth and leave it in a warm place to dry.

6. Resist the temptation to dismantle binoculars or telescopes, as this usually signals the beginning of the end of your optical equipment. Optical repairs specialists advertise in bird and photographic magazines.

Bird Photography

Taking good photographs of birds requires, above all, plenty of patience. Unlike buildings or people, birds have a strange habit of flying away, never to be seen again, just when you have got close enough to take a good photograph.

Digital SLR cameras are becoming cheaper and better all the time. For serious bird photography you will need a camera with interchangeable lenses. Generally, the bigger the lens the larger the magnification, weight and price. A lens of between 300mm and 500mm is the best for bird photography but can be very expensive. Also the size of the chip/sensor in your camera will determine how much you can enlarge your photo without it disappearing in a blizzard of pixels.

If you are not intending to enter your photos in competitions, when images may be scrutinised under a microscope, an increasingly popular and relatively inexpensive option is what is known as digiscoping and phonescoping. This involves using a telescope and putting a compact digital camera up to the eyepiece to take a photo through the telescope. There are many articles on the subject on the Internet, and with the right combination of telescope and camera you can get some amazing photographs without having to drag a camera and big lens as well as your telescope and binoculars around with you. Phonescoping is where you put the camera on your mobile phone up to the eyepiece of your telescope and you can take what is sometimes called a 'record

Digiscoping – with an adaptor for a pocket camera you can transform your telescope into a powerful lens. (Courtesy Opticron)

shot', a photo of acceptable quality that would help you identify an unusual bird later. You can even try using your digital camera or phone with your binoculars.

Getting to know the birds you want to photograph will help you get closer without disturbing them. A framed hide, while cumbersome to carry about, once set up will allow you to get very close pictures without a very powerful lens. Most of the world's top photographers take their best photos from hides. Another related accessory is a bag hide. This is basically a camouflaged bag or shroud to put over your head, which has openings that allow you to use your camera and avoids the trouble of having to erect a frame-supported hide. Stalking birds is also a very rewarding way to take good photographs, though the pain factor can increase enormously and the bird might fly away before you get close enough for a decent shot. Try crawling on one hand and two knees across even the smoothest of lawns while staying perfectly quiet. If you manage that then try crawling across a rocky beach or through nettle- and bramble-infested undergrowth. Not for everyone! A relatively easy way to get good pictures of birds is to photograph them coming to feeders, bird tables or birdbaths in the winter. With a tripod and an extension lead/remote control for the shutter release you can get close pictures with even a 50mm lens. You can cheat a little by placing a twig sticking out of the feeder or bird table that the birds can use as a perch. If you are careful to avoid including the feeder or table in the frame, the bird will look as if it is in a 'natural' environment. Anywhere birds have become used to people, such as in a park, duck-feeding areas, or where fish are processed, is good for taking photos of them.

When birdwatching, it is important to remember never to disturb the birds. This is very important during the breeding season, especially if they have young. In both Northern Ireland and the Republic of Ireland it is required by law to have a government licence to take or make photographic, video or other pictures of a protected wild bird on or near a nest containing eggs or unfledged young. Such licences can be applied for from the National Parks and Wildlife Service (NPWS) or Department of Environment Northern Ireland.

Tripods

A tripod is invaluable if you get a telescope, camera or video camera, allowing you to see and get steadier images and not be limited to the nearest wall, rock or fence post as a support. It is possible also to get an attachment for a tripod to take a pair of binoculars. This can be very handy as shake is eliminated and it frees the hands for note-taking, etc. Monopods, often seen being used by professional photographers at sports events, are less cumbersome than tripods though not as steady or versatile and are really suitable only for cameras and binoculars.

Finally, remember there might be other people watching the bird you are trying to photograph or film, so be considerate and ask their permission before trying to get a little closer. Also, respect people's privacy and private property. Restrain yourself from using any optical equipment on crowded beaches, or built-up areas. Remember, people might not realise that you are only interested in the bird on the hedge in their garden.

Birds and Conservation

Why conserve birds?

There are many reasons why we should conserve bird life. Firstly, birds play a very important part in the web of life on our planet. They provide us with food, beauty and inspiration and, within the food chain, they play a vital role, for example in helping to balance populations of 'pest' insects or in clearing carrion. Without birds our lives would be much duller! There are many ways in which you can help to conserve our birds and the special habitats in which they live. They are an important part of our natural heritage now and for the future.

The Corncrake, once a familiar sight and sound in the countryside, now stands on the verge of extinction in Ireland.

Through bird conservation our countryside's wild habitats will be retained, therefore, by conserving birds we also take care of the places where they live and the many other species of wildlife that co-exist in those places, covering almost every type of habitat you can think of, from the ocean to the mountains.

Birds and the law

Governments have come to realise that we need laws to avoid uncontrolled destruction of our wild creatures and their habitats. In the Republic of Ireland, birds are protected predominantly under the 1976 Wildlife Act, its subsequent amendments and a range of related regulations. In Northern Ireland, the 1985 Wildlife Order and associated legislation plays the same role. This legislation is similar in both parts of the island and is updated as circumstances for our birds and other wildlife continue to change. At present, all wild birds are protected by law, though for certain species 'seasons' are declared in which they can be hunted. In addition, a certain few species can legally be culled in situations where they are causing problems to agriculture, subject to the requirements laid down in the Wildlife Acts. Most duck species can be shot between 1 September and 31 January. Other 'game' species with a hunting season include Snipe, Pheasant and Red Grouse. All goose species are fully protected. Some species are regarded as pest species, e.g. Magpies, and can be legally killed more widely. Other species can be killed only under licence and if there is a proven need to do so such as where the health or safety of people is threatened, e.g. at airports.

In severe winter weather, when many birds may become very weak through cold and starvation, hunting may be stopped or suspended by ministerial order. The trapping of all wild birds is illegal. The only exceptions are when a licence is given to qualified bird-ringers for the purpose of studying birds which are released unharmed. Not very long ago the trapping of finches was a relatively common practice, with many houses having a caged linnet or goldfinch. Despite the fact that the majority of people now regard this as cruel and unnecessary, illegal trapping still continues. It is not illegal to have 'wild' bird species which are reared from captive stock. A significant function of BirdWatch Ireland and the RSPB is to ensure that the laws relating to wild birds are enforced by statutory agencies and, on occasion, to co-operate with the authorities in taking legal action against those who break these laws. Through the monitoring of bird populations they will also make recommendations for changes in the law if it is thought to be inadequate.

How can we help conserve birds?

At local level

Like many other things, bird conservation can begin at home. There are many things, at a personal or local level, that you can do to help birds in their daily lives:

1. Make your garden bird-friendly by planting suitable trees and plants such as berry bushes and by providing water, perhaps by making a permanent pond.

2. The plastic rings holding packs of beer or soft drink cans together can get caught around birds' necks and result in their suffering a long, slow, agonising death. Always cut up these plastic rings before throwing them in the bin and if you come across them bring them home or tear them up on the spot.

3. Discarded fishing line is another lethal trap for birds, so always cut the line up into small pieces before disposing of it in a waste bin. Also try to avoid using lead weights. Safe substitutes are available. Lost lead can find its way into Mute Swans and other wildfowl and poison them.

4. Under the Wildlife Acts, hedge-cutting in the Republic of Ireland is illegal between 1 March and 31 August each year, though some exceptions are allowed for, amongst others, reasons of road safety and agricultural operations. Please report any illegal hedge-cutting to the National Parks & Wildlife Service or your local authority.

If you live in the country or have land to manage, why not consider creating some valuable natural habitats such as woodland, wetlands or scrub, where appropriate? Advice can be sought from BirdWatch Ireland or the RSPB on how to go about this.

5. Look around your area and identify small ponds, stands of trees or other 'wild' areas (unfortunately referred to by some as 'wasteland'), if possible, get a map and mark them in and write a short letter to your local authority, outlining the importance of these areas for wildlife. Ask them to keep your submission on file for future reviews of their development plan for your area. Local authorities welcome such infor-mation as it makes them aware of your concern for these sites. They might not seem very important at present but, as other areas are destroyed, their value will increase greatly with time.

The golden rule in local conservation is never to wait until a site comes under threat to try and save it, as this may be too late. Don't wait for someone else to protect your environment, because they probably won't. Any arguments for saving a wildlife area should always be backed by strong evidence or data. Contact BirdWatch Ireland or the RSPB and ask their advice. The area in which you are interested may have been included in a survey at some time in the past and any information on its wildlife value would strengthen your case. Unfortunately, in this age of budgets and cash-strapped local authorities, arguments based solely on emotion will rarely save 'your' site.

At national level

Bird conservation at national level is similar to that at local level but on a larger scale. You are dealing with many interested parties, all with different concerns in vying for the same piece of land for totally different purposes. The best way to contribute to national bird and wildlife conservation is to join BirdWatch Ireland in the Republic of Ireland or the RSPB in Northern Ireland. The larger the membership of such organisations the more they will be listened to by decision-makers who, in turn, can influence policies and legis-lation in relation to conservation.

BirdWatch Ireland and RSPB NI have agreed a list of priority bird species for conservation action on the island of Ireland. These Birds of Conservation Concern in Ireland (BoCCI) are published in a list known as the BoCCI List. In it, birds are classified into three separate lists (Red, Amber and Green), based on the conservation status of the bird and hence conservation priority.

The **Red List** birds are of high conservation concern, the **Amber List** birds are of medium conservation concern and the **Green List** birds are not considered threatened. Specific criteria are used to classify a bird into one of these three categories.

Birds of Conservation Concern in Ireland (BoCCI)

Ireland's Most Threatened Bird Species

The Red List

Breeding Species
Barn Owl
Black-headed Gull
Black-necked Grebe
Common Scoter
Corncrake
Curlew
Golden Eagle
Golden Plover
Grey Partridge
Hen Harrier
Herring Gull
Lapwing
Nightjar
Quail
Red Grouse
Red-necked Phalarope
Redshank
Ring Ouzel
Roseate Tern
Twite
Yellowhammer

Wintering Populations
Balearic Shearwater
Bewick's Swan
Knot
Pintail
Shoveler
Sooty Shearwater

Other species for which Ireland is especially important but which are currently on the amber list include: Barnacle and Greenland White-fronted Goose, Manx Shearwater, Roseate Tern, Storm Petrel and Whooper Swan.

Ireland also has a range of threatened bird habitats. Perhaps the most significant of these are the lowland wet grassland or callows, the machair grasslands (sandy coastal lowlands), raised and blanket bogs, fens and other wetlands, intertidal flats, salt marshes and coastal lagoons and, of course, our open ocean.

At international level

Because birds can fly and do not recognise political boundaries they are the best example to show the need for a global approach to wildlife conservation. Ireland plays host to hundreds of thousands of birds which spend part of their year in another country, often very far away and necessitating a flight that will take them across many countries. For example, the Swallow, which comes to Ireland each summer to raise its young, undertakes a hazardous journey to reach here. Apart from having to survive the winter months south of the Sahara, it will, when it starts its migration in spring, first have to endure the harsh conditions over the Sahara desert. If it succeeds, it will face sea crossings and illegal hunting over the Mediterranean before eventually returning to Ireland. Similarly, geese that are protected in Ireland are shot in other countries on their way south to winter here each year. If we want birds such as the Swallow to return to us each summer, it is vital that international co-operation between governments is encouraged. Many international treaties already exist to protect birds, such as the European Communities Directive on the Conservation of Wild Birds and the Council of Europe Convention on the Conservation of European Wildlife and Natural Habitats (also known as the Bern Convention). Birdlife International (of which BirdWatch Ireland is the representative in the Republic and the RSPB in Northern Ireland) is the organisation dedicated to the conservation of wild birds throughout the world. It promotes conservation plans and direct action which include local initiatives to protect globally and regionally endangered bird species and habitats. By joining BirdWatch Ireland or the RSPB you will be supporting bird conservation at an international level.

How To Use This Guide

Apart from a few exceptions, only species recorded more than 300 times in Ireland are dealt with in this guide. They are grouped into two categories: Common, and Scarce & Rare species. Many identification guides arrange species in strict scientific or taxonomic order. For most birdwatchers bird identification relies on a bird's visual and aural characteristics as well as its preferred habitat, rather than its internal anatomy or DNA profile. To help with the visual identification process, the various species groups in this guide are, where possible, arranged by visual similarity and habitat preference rather than scientific order.

The Bird Photographs

The photos in the species profiles have been selected to help you identify the species in different plumages. Birds are rarely seen in neutral light and more usually seen in light conditions such as shade, bright sunshine, in silhouette, etc. The colours of the birds on a species plate may vary but all are within natural observed variations. Colour descriptions in the accompanying text are for neutral light. It is beyond the scope of this guide to include photos of every plumage type; the images shown should be enough to identify the species in question.

Common Species Profiles

All the common species are treated with a full page of images and identification notes and, where possible, bird species that look similar are grouped together. Those included as 'common' are birds that can be seen relatively easily in Ireland, if you are in the right habitat and at the right time of year. This means that a bird like the Puffin is included: although rarely seen on mainland Ireland, where suitable nesting habitat is available they are common. Red Kite and Great Spotted Woodpecker, while currently not common species, are increasing in numbers and have been included to make people aware of them.

Scarce & Rare Species Profiles

Where appropriate, at the end of the descriptions of each group of common birds, relevant scarce and rare birds are shown. They are represented by one or two images with a brief description. These species are ones that are not regularly found in Ireland but are included to make you aware of the possibility of finding one of them. Almost all are birds that have strayed from their normal range. Often they are similar to common species in that group and, if this is the case, a page reference will be made to that common species.

Species Profiles

As this is an identification guide, only useful identification features are described to help the reader to separate one species from another. The features given in the text and indicated by pointer arrows on the photographs are the essential ones to see to be sure of your identification. Some individual features will be shared with other species, but the combination of features described in the text and pointed out on the images will rarely, if ever, be shared with other species. Pointer arrows are also used to indicate features which separate male from female or which should identify the bird's age. Information on those species given a full page is presented as follows:

Species Profile Page

Information Bar
(see p. 32)

Robin | Spideóg | *Erithacus rubecula*
L 13–14cm WS 21cm AY CB Farmland/Garden/Woodland

Adult: bright red-orange breast; grey forehead, side of the neck and upper breast; white belly; warm brown upperparts; stands upright; round appearance. **Juv/Im:** young birds, just out of the nest do not have a red breast, but instead are scaled light and dark brown; buff spots and streaks on the back and wings. **In flight:** flies fast and straight. **Voice:** call is a loud, thin ptic, usually repeated several times, often out of sight. It sings all year round but is at its loudest during spring, when its melodious twittering is often performed from a fence post or a prominent bush.

Abbreviations used in the species profiles

M.	Male
F.	Female
Br.	Breeding plumage
NBr.	Non-breeding plumage
Juv.	Juvenile plumage
Im.	Immature plumage
1st W.	1st winter plumage
1st S.	1st summer plumage
1st Y.	1st year plumage
2nd W.	2nd winter plumage
2nd S.	2nd summer plumage
3rd W.	3rd winter plumage
3rd S.	3rd summer plumage
4th W.	4th winter plumage
Ad.	Adult

See p. 35 for more information on these abbreviations.

Abbreviations used in the information bar

L	Length
WS	Wingspan
AY	Can be seen all year round
Su	Usually seen in summer
A	Usually seen in autumn
Sp	Usually seen in spring
W	Usually seen in winter
CB	Common Breeding Species
SB	Scarce Breeding Species
RB	Rare Breeding Species
NB	Non-Breeding Species

See p. 33 for more information on these abbreviations.

Information Bar

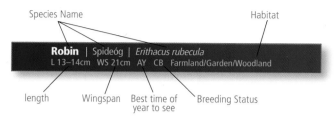

Species Name   Habitat

Robin | Spideóg | *Erithacus rubecula*
L 13–14cm   WS 21cm   AY   CB   Farmland/Garden/Woodland

length   Wingspan   Best time of   Breeding Status
                           year to see

Species name: the English names used are the 'traditional' ones which are most familiar to people in Ireland, followed by the name in the Irish language and then the scientific (usually Latin) name in *italics*. With the explosion in book publication in the last 100 years and the advent of rapid means of communication such as the Internet, English has increasingly become an international language of communication, which has led to a need to standardise the English names of birds. As most of the English names we use today come from Britain or America, a lot of the standard English bird names have no adjective because there was only one species of that type in Britain and/or North America. Examples include 'cormorant', 'kingfisher' and 'snipe', terms originally used to describe a specific species, although in the northern hemisphere alone there are 12 different species with the word cormorant, eight with snipe and 13 with kingfisher in their name. In order to standardise the English names of birds like these and avoid confusion for those using English to discuss or write about birds, an organisation called the International Ornithologists' Union (IOU) recently produced a standard list of English names. We have included these names in brackets in the contents page.

Length (L): is expressed in centimetres and represents an average adult measurement or range of measurements of the species when dead and laid out straight, from the tip of the beak to the middle of the end of the tail. So for long-tailed species like Magpie or Long-tailed Tit, whose tails are as long as their bodies, their body size will be a lot smaller than a bird of similar length with a short tail such as a gull. Remember, these measurements are only a guide and individual birds with measurements outside of those given will always turn up. Some measurement ranges may seem very wide; this is often because there is a noticeable size difference between the male and female and/or across their global breeding range. For example, male birds of prey are usually noticeably smaller than females.

Wingspan (WS): is expressed in centimetres and represents an average adult measurement or range of measurements of the bird from wing tip to wing tip.

Best time to see (AY = All Year; Su = Summer; A = Autumn; Sp = Spring; W = Winter): this will give you a good idea of what time of year you are *most likely* to see the species in question. As already mentioned, birds do not read bird identification books, so there is always the possibility of seeing or hearing a species outside these times. All the common birds in this book can appear in almost all months of the year, including most of those we consider just summer or winter visitors. Many, such as the Robin (**AY**), are common and widely distributed and seen all year round. Others such as the Swallow (**Sp/Su/A**) usually arrive in spring (**Sp**), are common and widely distributed during the summer (**Su**) and leave in autumn (**A**). Many of our wetland birds, such as the Wigeon (**A/W/Sp**), arrive in early autumn (**A**), are commonly found in winter (**W**) and depart in spring (**Sp**). Some species that breed here in relatively small numbers, such as the Redshank, are joined by others from abroad in the winter. If you are lucky enough to live in an area of Ireland where they breed you might see them all year round or only during the summer, but most of us will usually only see them away from the breeding grounds in autumn, winter and spring, so we use (**A/W/Sp**) for a species like this.

Breeding Status: the following codes are a representative way of illustrating the breeding status of the species in Ireland as a whole.

CB = Common Breeding: birds that are a widespread breeding species in suitable habitat, such as Robin, Rook, Guillemot (at seabird colonies), etc.

SB = Scarce Breeding: birds that are a breeding species in relatively small numbers in suitable habitat, for example, Chough, Red Grouse, Whinchat, Lapwing, Cuckoo, Little Egret.

RB = Rare Breeding: birds that breed in very small numbers, as few as two or three pairs on the whole island, in suitable habitat. Examples are Red-throated Diver, Corncrake, Hen Harrier, Redstart, Wood Warbler.

NB = Non-Breeding: birds that are not known to breed here, are seasonal and usually come to Ireland outside the breeding season, such as the Brent Goose, which arrives here in the autumn after breeding and departs in spring. This category also includes non-breeding birds, such as the Whimbrel, which pass through in good numbers on spring or autumn migration. It also includes scarce or rare visitors which do not breed here (as far as we know) such as the Ring-billed Gull from North America, which occurs annually but in very small numbers.

Habitat: this describes where the bird is *usually* found in Ireland and may help with identification. If more than one habitat is given, they are listed in order of where you are most likely to find them. Having said that, birds can turn up in the most unlikely habitats, well away from where they are typically found. After storms, for instance, Gannets, which usually stay well out to sea, have turned up in fields and on ponds quite far inland. Some species spend the breeding season in one habitat and use different habitats outside the breeding season. Kingfishers generally breed on freshwater rivers but can be seen in estuaries and on the coast in winter. Be very cautious, but never rule out identifying a species based on where you see it. The habitat types used in the species accounts are:

Sea: mainly at sea, usually away from the coast.

Coast: mainly along the coast, sandy or rocky shore, and associated habitats such as cliffs, coastal grassland, sand dune and lagoon.

Estuary: where a river enters the sea and the water is mainly saltwater and tidal. Also associated habitats such as mudflat and saltmarsh, etc.

Wetland: all freshwater habitats such as stream, river, lake, and associated habitats such as reed bed, bog, canal and man-made ponds, etc.

Farmland: any cultivated land, tillage, grassland, hedgerows, and associated habitats such as fallow land and uncultivated meadow, etc.

Woodland: any substantial natural, semi-natural or planted deciduous, coniferous or mixed wooded area, and associated habitat such as understorey growth, etc.

Upland: any area of high ground free of trees or shrubs.

Garden: any garden, big or small, rural, suburban or urban.

Suburban: a mixture of moderate housing density and gardens.

Urban: High-density housing with few gardens and associated parks, etc.

The Species Identification Notes
Notes are given at the bottom of each plate on key identification features when the bird is seen on the ground or on water, followed

by key identification features when in flight. Birds can have vivid patterns on their wings which are hidden when the wings are folded. As far as possible, the identification features are arranged in order of importance.

Describing the bird: the plumage on a bird is very complex but it can usually be divided into fairly consistent feather groups or areas. It would be almost impossible to write the species descriptions in this guide without using standard terms to describe various parts of the bird and its plumage. Some of these might sound like unnecessary jargon but they are tried and tested. By looking through this book regularly with reference to the parts of the bird illustrated on pp. 4–5, you will quickly become familiar with these terms. While you can use whatever terms you like for yourself, when it comes to describing the bird to someone else, a common language of description is essential.

Size: apart from giving the length and wingspan in centimetres, an indication of the size of a bird is given wherever possible by making a comparison with a well-known bird. As birds in this guide vary in size from a couple of centimetres to over a metre, when describing the size of different parts of the bird such as beak, eye, legs, neck, etc., terms are used relative to the overall size of the bird. The beak of a Mute Swan, for instance, is not very long for the size of the bird but would be huge on a Robin!

Sexes similar: where the plumage of the male and female is similar, this term is used. There may be small differences in appearance but they are usually noticeable only at close range.

Colour: the plumage colours in the species descriptions are a relatively subjective guide, as a bird's plumage can look different in different light conditions, and what one person calls chestnut-brown another might call red-brown. In this book, when a colour description like 'pinkish-white' is used this means that the colour is mainly white with a pink tinge. If 'orange-brown' is used it means the colour is thought to be roughly an equal mix of orange and brown. The image plates will help give a good idea of plumage colour.

Male (M.)/Female (F.): where the male and female have significantly different plumage (e.g. ducks and finches), the male is described first, followed by the female, with any differences from the male plumage highlighted.

Br/NBr (Breeding plumage/Non-breeding plumage): some species, especially the waders, only differ significantly in appearance during the breeding season. Where there are significant differences the birds are described separately, with the male first followed by the female, with any differences from the male plumage highlighted. Most adult birds acquire breeding plumage through moult and/or feather wear any time from February/March onwards and may still be in breeding plumage at the end of September. Most adult birds are in non-breeding plumage between October and February.

Eclipse plumage: some male birds, especially the ducks, have plumages which they acquire for a short time after breeding through what is called a post-breeding moult. This plumage is called 'eclipse plumage' and can make males appear very similar to the female of the species.

Age by plumage appearance: most birds cannot be aged based on plumage appearance once they acquire full adult plumage. Some, such as gulls, can usually be aged on their plumage appearance before this. The following headings are used to describe birds in age-specific plumage: **Juv** refers to distinctive juvenile plumage shortly after fledging. Gulls and some other species will be in immature (Im) plumage for up to four years. More specifically, such species can be aged as follows: 1st winter, 1st summer, 2nd winter, 2nd summer, 3rd winter, 3rd summer, etc. This language describes a plumage associated with a bird of a particular age, before reaching adult plumage, i.e. **1st winter** would be a bird in its first winter after hatching; **1st summer** is the first full summer after hatching, approximately a year old and in its second calendar year; and **3rd year** would be a bird in its third calendar year after hatching. **Im** refers to plumage of immature birds not yet in full adult plumage but which cannot be aged with confidence.

In flight: this describes key identification patterns and colours seen when the bird is in flight as well as any useful information such as flight pattern (straight, undulating, etc.) and flight behaviour (gliding or hovering, etc.).

Voice: notes on calls and songs are given only if they are distinctive and might help to identify a bird. Phonetic description of bird sounds is very subjective and so is only a very rough guideline. Taking time to stop and listen to the songs and calls of the common birds you can identify by sight is the best way of developing your bird-sound identification skills. You will then learn to detect new and unusual birds by sound. For recordings of bird sounds, check www.xeno-canto.org or the BirdWatch Ireland shop which has a number of CDs of bird sounds.

Maps: species distribution maps for Ireland are not included as they have limited value for bird identification.

Ireland is a relatively small area of land and the distribution of most common species corresponds generally to the distribution of suitable habitats.

Swans, Geese and Ducks

This group of water birds is well represented in Ireland. The ducks can be divided into two main groups: those that feed from the surface of the water, sometimes called 'dabbling ducks', such as Mallard and Teal, and those that dive underwater to catch their food, such as the Tufted Duck. They have a broad-ranging diet with some species being almost totally vegetarian while others are mainly fish-eaters. We have three regularly occurring geese in Ireland. The Wexford Wildfowl Refuge on Wexford's North Slob is internationally important for the Greenland White-fronted Goose, emblem of BirdWatch Ireland. Each winter over 40 per cent of the total world population of this species comes to the reserve. We have three swan species in Ireland: the well-known Mute Swan and the less well-known Whooper and Bewick's Swans, which are winter visitors and often referred to as wild swans. In recent years the Bewick's Swan has become a scarce visitor to Ireland. As well as seeing our native birds you might come across an escaped or feral bird. These are usually exotic species from faraway places that are kept in waterfowl collections both private and public. Some of these are included in this section as they occasionally escape from captivity and may be seen here in the wild.

Shelduck

Mute Swan | Eala bhalbh | *Cygnus olor*
L 130–155cm WS 200–230cm AY CB Wetland/Estuary

Very big. **Adult**: all white, occasionally stained pink/brown in parts; orange and black beak with black knob (bigger on male); on ground/swimming, note curved neck. **Juv**: cygnet downy grey with all-dark beak; **1ˢᵗ W**: pink-and-black beak with little or no knob; pale grey-brown plumage turning white towards end of winter/beginning of spring. **In flight**: long neck held straight out; the wings make a buzzing sound; on take-off, runs along the surface of water with powerful wingbeats. **Voice**: greeting call is a soft wheezing *whe-aarrrr*, also lower coughing sounds. (See Whooper Swan p. 39, Bewick's Swan p. 59.)

Mute Swan

† W.

Ad.

Ad.

cygnets

1st W.

Whooper Swan | Eala ghlórach | *Cygnus cygnus*
L 145–160cm WS 225–235cm A/W/Sp RB Wetland/Farmland

Size of Mute Swan; sexes similar; neck is held relatively straight on standing/swimming birds. **Adult**: all white but can become stained on head/neck; yellow-and-black wedge-shaped beak; yellow usually extends beyond nostril/towards tip and varies in extent; no knob on beak. **1st W**: pale yellow and pink on beak, pale grey-brown plumage becoming whiter as winter progresses. **In flight**: looks pale with long neck outstretched; often flies in a loose V-formation. **Voice**: unlike Mute Swan, can be very vocal making high-pitched whooping/trumpeting sound like out-of-tune wind instrument. (See Mute Swan p. 38, Bewick's Swan p. 59.)

Ad.

Ad.

1st W.

Greenland White-fronted Goose | Gé bhánéadanach | *Anser albifrons*
L 68–74cm   WS 135–155cm   A/W/Sp   NB   Farmland/Wetland

Smaller than farmyard goose; beak usually orange, occasionally pink; orange legs.
Adult: white forehead and white border around base of beak; dark blotches on
belly. From a distance, looks dark brown with white vent/undertail coverts. **1st W**:
lacks dark blotches on belly; white on the head is absent or reduced. **In flight**: dark
blotches on belly of adults; dark brown back/secondary wing coverts; thin indistinct
pale wing bars; white rump/dark tail with thin white edge; white around beak on
adults. **Voice**: high-pitched clarinet-like cackling sounds. (See Greylag Goose p. 41,
Pink-footed Goose p. 59, Bean Goose p. 59.)

Greylag Goose | Gé ghlas | *Anser anser*
L 85cm WS 155cm All year SB (feral birds only) Wetland

Larger and greyer than Greenland White-fronted Goose, p. 40. **All ages**: stout, conical, all-pink or orange beak; pink legs; usually does not look dark headed; large area of the wing pale grey, only visible when the wing is stretched or in flight. Feral populations breed in parts of the country so birds seen, especially in the south, may not be true wild birds, particularly in summer. In Ireland wild Greylag Geese winter in the northern half of the island. (See Greenland White-fronted Goose p. 40, Bean Goose p. 59, Pink-footed Goose p. 59.)

Barnacle Goose | Gé ghiúrainn | *Branta leucopsis*
L 60–70cm WS 130–140cm A/W/Sp NB Coast/Farmland

A bit bigger than a Curlew; legs and short beak are black; sexes similar. **All ages**: creamy-white face and black head, throat and breast; black-and-white body. **In flight**: creamy-white face and black neck and breast, light grey wings with a dark trailing edge. Usually seen in flocks on the northwest coast but individuals can turn up anywhere. **Voice**: like a small dog barking. (See also Canada Goose p. 62, Brent Goose p. 43.)

Ad.

v./1st W.

Ad. with colour rings

Brent Goose | Gé dhubh/Cadhan | *Branta bernicula*
L 58–62cm WS 115–125cm A/W/Sp NB Estuary/suburban parks/playing pitches

Smaller than farmyard goose; legs/short beak black. **Adult**: black head/neck/breast; white 'gill' marks on side of neck; upperparts dark grey-brown; white tail with narrow black edge; undertail white; belly light grey-brown. **1ˢᵗ W**: similar to adult; less obvious white neck marks; white edges to wing feathers, narrow white wing bars. **In flight**: looks all dark except white on tail/under-tail – very noticeable. Fast wingbeats; usually flies in long, loose lines or bunched groups, often low over water. **Voice**: In flocks a muted, guttural quivering *grrough*/often silent on own. (See Barnacle Goose p. 42, Canada Goose p. 62.)

Shelduck | Lacha bhreach | *Tadorna tadorna*
L 58–71cm   WS 110–133cm   AY   CB   Estuary

Surface feeder; bigger than Mallard; found in estuaries, preferring mudflats. **Adult male**: mainly white body; black head/belly; red beak/pink legs; chestnut breast band – rules out any other duck. **Adult female**: smaller than male, no red knob on base of beak; little black on belly. **1st W**: similar shape to adult but is black and white, lacking bright colours. **In flight**: broad, pale chestnut breast band; black 'braces' on white back; black primaries/secondaries. **Voice**: usually vocal only during breeding season, including rapid guttural, laughing *agh-agh-agh-agh* lasting several seconds. Also high, liquid *tiew-tiew* with high whistle. (See Eider p. 53.)

Wigeon | Lacha rua | *Anas penelope*
L 45–51cm   WS 75–86cm   A/W/Sp   RB   Wetland/Estuary

Surface feeder; smaller than Mallard; short/black-tipped blue-grey beak; short grey legs. **Male:** dark red-brown head; conspicuous creamy forehead/crown. Mainly grey body; grey-pink breast; grey flanks; white belly; white patch at rear of flanks; black undertail coverts/vent. Male in eclipse plumage resembles female but retains white wing patches. **Female:** duller grey-brown with pale belly. **In flight**: white wing patches (male); both male/female have dark green speculum, unmarked pale underwing. Rises quickly when taking to air. **Voice**: male utters distinctive high-pitched whistling *feeoow* which can be heard at some distance; female makes lower guttural sound. (See American Wigeon p. 59, Similar Female Ducks p. 57.)

Mallard | Lacha fhiáin | *Anas platyrhynchos*
L 58–62cm   WS 81–95cm   AY   CB   Wetland/Estuary

A big surface feeding duck. **Male**: white neck ring; iridescent green-blue head; yellow beak; up-curled feathers at base of whitish tail. Male in eclipse plumage resembles female except yellow-green beak. **Female**: dull brown; beak reddish-orange and dark brown; lacks curled tail feathers. **In flight**: *male* – dark head, neck ring, white bordered blue speculum; *female* – brown; pale-edged tail; white-bordered blue/purple speculum. Rises almost vertically from water. Rapid wingbeats, direct flight. **Voice**: female makes wide variety of calls ranging from *quack* to what sounds like a laugh. Male makes a quiet *wheep* sound. (See Similar Female Ducks p. 57.)

Gadwall | Gadual | *Anas strepera*
L 48–54cm   WS 80–90cm   A/W/Sp   RB   Wetland

A surface feeder; smaller than Mallard; sits high on the water. **Male**: white speculum, not always visible; grey head and body; black around and under the tail; dark beak; pale yellow-orange legs; not as colourful as other male surface-feeding ducks. **Female**: resembles female Mallard but is greyer on the head; distinctive white speculum on the wing; more orange-sided dark beak than female Mallard. **In flight**: both male and female have white speculum; white underwing coverts and pale belly; no other obvious markings. Direct flight with rapid wingbeats. (See Similar Female Ducks p. 57.)

Teal | Praslacha | *Anas crecca*
L 34–38cm WS 58–64cm A/W/Sp SB Wetland/Estuary

Our smallest surface feeder, much smaller than Mallard. **Male**: chestnut head/neck; dark green eyepatch with thin buff edging extending down side of neck; pale yellow undertail outlined in black, horizontal white line above closed wing; in eclipse plumage resembles female. **Female**: scaly grey-brown; green speculum; short, pale, horizontal line under tail. **1ˢᵗ W**: similar to female. **In flight**: green speculum; pale wing bar; rises quickly when disturbed, rapid wingbeats, plain appearance. **Voice**: in winter, can be very noisy. Male makes a short high-pitched *krreet*; female makes much higher *quack*. (See Green-winged Teal p. 59, Similar Female Ducks p. 57.)

Pintail | Biorearrach | *Anas acuta*
L 57–59cm WS 87–89cm A/W/Sp RB Wetland/Estuary

Mallard-sized surface feeder; short blue-grey and black beak; relatively long, thin neck. **Male**: long, pointed tail; chocolate-brown head; thin white line running up side of neck. In eclipse plumage resembles female, quite grey/brown in appearance. **Female**: brown with shorter, pointed tail; all-grey beak; noticeably paler than female mallard. **In flight**: dark head; white breast/belly/long tail (on male); dark green speculum bordered by pale brown/white. Rises quickly from water or land. **Voice**: usually quiet, sounds like Mallard. The male makes squeaking *whee-hee* call, rising in pitch in the middle; female makes low quacking sounds. (See Similar Female Ducks p. 57.)

Shoveler | Spadalach | *Anas clypeata*
L 45–50cm WS 75–80cm AY RB Wetland/Estuary

Surface feeder; bit smaller than Mallard; oversized broad beak, black on male/dark brown with orange sides on female/1ˢᵗ W; orange legs; sits very low in water. **Male**: dark green head; chestnut flanks/belly. Eclipse male becomes duller. **Female**: brown; plain. **1ˢᵗ W**: resembles female/male in moult but darker overall. **In flight**: *male* – broad, pale blue inner wing patches; green speculum; dark head/chestnut belly; *female* – bluish-grey inner wing patches; green speculum lacks white trailing edge; rises vertically off water; direct flight with rapid wingbeats. **Voice**: usually silent, males make thin-sounding *seep* call; females make laughing *quack*. (See Similar Female Ducks p. 57.)

M.

M.

M.

F.

M.

F.

M.

Br. F.

duckling

Pochard | Póiseard | *Aythya farina*
L 44–48cm WS 70–77cm A/W/Sp RB Wetland/Estuary

Diving duck; smaller than Mallard. **Male**: chestnut-red head, black breast; grey body; black on rump/undertail coverts; red eye; dark beak with broad pale blue band. Duller in eclipse. **Female**: overall dark grey-brown; dark beak with pale blue patch towards tip; in non-breeding, greyer on body; dark eye. **1ˢᵗ W**: resembles females but browner/all-dark beak. **In flight**: *male*: grey back; grey wing with pale grey stripe; chestnut red head, black breast; pale belly/underwing; *female* appears dull; pale primaries with dark trailing edge. **Voice**: usually silent in winter. In breeding season male makes a variety of high-pitched, squeaky calls, guttural sounds, gentle *murrr*. (See Similar Female Ducks p. 57.)

F.

M. (moulting).

F.

F.

chick

M.

F.

Tufted Duck | Lacha bhadánach/Lacha dhubh | *Aythya fuligula*
L 40–47cm WS 67–73cm AY CB Wetland/Estuary

Small diving duck, noticeably smaller than Mallard. **Male**: long tuft of black feathers sticking out of back of the head; all black with white belly/flanks; purple-blue sheen on black feathers visible at close range; light blue-grey beak, black tip; bright golden-yellow eye. **Female**: short, blunt tuft, dark brown; pale belly; varying degrees of paleness around base of beak. **I**st **W**: similar to female but tuft almost absent. **In flight**: fast, straight; broad white wing bar; white belly/underwing. **Voice**: usually silent; in courtship male makes quiet whistling sound. Female makes growling sound. (See Scaup p. 60, Ring-necked Duck p. 60, Similar Female Ducks p. 57.)

Juv.

Ad. M.

Ad. F.

M. (moulting)

Ad. M.

Ad. F.

Ad. F.

Ad. F.

Ad. F.

M. (moulting)

Ad. F.

Eider | Éadar | *Somateria mollissima*
L 60–65cm WS 94–98cm AY SB Coast/Sea

Large diving duck; a bit bigger than Mallard; stout wedge-shaped beak. **Male:** black cap with lime green on nape/side of neck; overall white upperparts/black underside. **Female:** all brown, heavily barred light/dark brown. 1st W: similar to female but not as heavily barred, pale supercilium. Compared to adult breeding male, 1st S male and males in moult have more dark feathers on breast/back. **In flight:** *male* has white back and inner-wing area; black outer wing, tail and belly. *Female* all brown. **Voice:** male makes a soft *cuu-aawe* sound and females make a sharper gull-like *gaup* sound. (See Shelduck p. 44, Similar Female Ducks p. 57.)

Common Scoter | Scótar | *Melanitta nigra*
L 47–51cm   WS 80–84cm   A/W/Sp   RB   Sea/Coast

A diving duck, usually seen from coast; smaller than Mallard. **Male**: all black, dark beak with orange-yellow patch on upper mandible and knob at base. **Female**: dark crown, pale grey cheek; dark brown body, almost all-dark grey beak. **1st W**: similar to female. All dark with pale belly. Young males have no knob at base of beak. **In flight**: looks all dark with pale sheen to underwing feathers in some light conditions. **Voice**: usually silent outside the breeding season. Usually seen in flocks at sea outside the breeding season. Breeds on freshwater lakes. (See Velvet Scoter p. 59.)

Goldeneye | Órshúileach | *Bucephala clangula*
L 42–46cm   WS 66–76cm   A/W/Sp   NB   Wetland/Estuary

Diving duck; smaller than Mallard. **Male**: large oval white spot at base of dark beak, large iridescent green head which can look purple or black depending on light; looks black and white at a distance. Golden-yellow iris; orange-yellow legs; eclipse plumage resembles female but retains some of its white face patch and is paler. **Female**: no white face patch; white neck collar, red-brown head, grey body; white wing feathers showing towards tail; pale pink-orange patch near tip of dark beak. I^st W: resemble females but browner overall; all-dark beak. **In flight**: large, white wing patches; black on underwing; high forehead/crown; rapid direct flight. (See Similar Female Ducks p. 57)

Red-breasted Merganser | Síolta rua | *Mergus serrator*
L 53–57cm WS 70–80cm A/W/Sp SB Estuary/Wetland

Diving duck; slightly smaller than a Mallard; long, thin red beak; red legs; red eye.
Male: long, spiky feathers sticking out of the back of its dark green head; white
neck; dark-streaked pale chestnut breast; variable amounts of white visible on the
closed wing. **Female:** pale reddish-brown head, light shaggy crest; red-brown on
back of the neck fading to pale grey on the front, grey-brown body. **In flight:** fast
and straight with rapid wingbeats; large, white inner-wing patches on the male,
smaller on the female; stretched neck appearance. **Voice:** usually silent. (See
Goosander p. 60, Similar Female Ducks p. 57.)

Similar Female Ducks

Pintail

Teal

Mallard

Wigeon

Gadwall

Red-breasted Merganser

Shoveler

Eider

Goldeneye

Pochard

Tufted Duck

Note: Images not to scale

Scarce & Rare

Bean Goose | Síolghé | *Anser fabalis*
L 68–86cm   WS 145–172cm   W   NB   Farmland/Wetland
Similar to Greenland White-fronted Goose (p. 40) but slightly bigger and lacks white on head. **Adult:** dark beak with a pink-orange patch near the tip that in 1st W usually tapers to a point at the base of the beak; orange legs; narrow white terminal band to dark tail; looks dark headed.

Pink-footed Goose | Gé ghobghearr | *Anser brachyrhynchus*
L 66–74cm   WS 140–160cm   W   NB   Farmland/Wetland
Similar in size and appearance to Greenland White-fronted Goose, p. 40. **Adult:** dark beak with a pale pink patch; pink legs; pale grey on the wings; broad white terminal band to dark tail; looks dark headed.

Bewick's Swan | Eala Bewick | *Cygnus columbianus*
L 118–126cm   WS 172–193cm   W   NB   Wetland
Similar to Whooper Swan p. 39 but smaller. **Adult:** less yellow on the beak, never coming past the nostril.

American Wigeon | Lacha rua Mheiriceánach | *Anas americana*
L 48–54cm   WS 78–90cm   A/W/Sp   NB   Wetland/Estuary
Surface-feeding duck, similar in size and appearance to Eurasian Wigeon, p. 45 female/1st W difficult to identify and separate from female Eurasian Wigeon. **Adult male:** creamy-white forehead and crown; green eyepatch extending back to the base of the nape; dark cream cheeks with dark speckles; pink-grey back, breast and flanks.

Garganey | Praslacha shamhraidh | *Anas querquedula*
L 38–40cm   WS 60–66cm   A/W/Sp   RB   Wetland
Surface-feeding duck; slightly bigger than Eurasian Teal, p. 48. **Male:** dark head and breast, broad white supercilium extending back to the base of the nape; no obvious green speculum; in flight: pale grey wing patches. **Female:** hard to tell from female Eurasian Teal; pale spot at base of beak; darker eye stripe and paler supercilium, the face looks striped.

Green-winged Teal | Praslacha Mheiriceánach | *Anas carolinensis*
L 34–38cm   WS 53–58cm   A/W/Sp   NB   Wetland/Estuary
Similar in size and appearance to Eurasian Teal, p. 48. **Male:** vertical white line on side of breast, no white horizontal line above flanks on resting bird. **Female:** almost impossible to separate from Eurasian Teal.

Velvet Scoter | Sceadach | *Melanitta fusca*
L 52–58cm   WS 80–95cm   W   NB   Coast
Diving duck, similar to Common Scoter, p. 54; white wing patch, not always visible when on the water. Yellow patch near base of beak on M. Unlike Common Scoter it half opens its wings when diving.

Bean Goose

Pink-footed Goose

Bewick's Swan

American Wigeon (M.)

Teal (F.)

Garganey (F.)

Garganey (M.)

Green-winged Teal (M.)

Ad. M.

Velvet Scoter

Note: Images not to scale

Scarce & Rare *(cont'd)*

Smew | Síolta gheal | *Mergellus albellus*
L 38–44cm   WS 56–68cm   W   NB   Estuary/Coast

Diving duck, same size as Shoveler, p. 50. **Male**: black, grey and white; black patch between the eye and beak. **Female**: foxy-red head (also known as Redhead), white throat and grey body; in flight: white patches on inner wing.

Goosander | Síolta mhór | *Mergus merganser*
L 57–68cm   WS 80–92cm   W   RB   Wetland/Estuary

Similar to Red-breasted Merganser (p. 56) but larger. **Male**: dark head and neck and pinkish-white breast and belly. **Female:** white chin; straight, sharp divide between brown head and neck and pale breast.

Ring-necked Duck | Lacha mhuinceach | *Aythya collaris*
L 38–45cm   WS 62cm   W   NB   Wetland

Similar to Tufted Duck (p. 52) but with differences such as its distinctive head shape, pointed towards the rear of the crown. **Male:** like male Tufted Duck but with white band near tip of beak, light grey flank with vertical white patch between grey flank and black breast. Female: browner, same peak shape as male and pale eye ring.

Scaup | Lacha iascán | *Aythya marila*
L 42–50cm   WS 72–79cm   W   NB   Coast/Estuary

Diving duck; resembles Tufted Duck (p. 52) but without tuft. **Male:** differs from male Tufted Duck by pale grey back. **Female:** greyer back than female Tufted Duck and usually large white border to the base of the beak.

Long-tailed Duck | Lacha earrfhada | *Clangula hyemalis*
L 40–48cm (excluding tail)   WS 66–80cm   W   NB   Coast/Estuary

A diving duck about the size of a Tufted Duck, p. 52. **Male:** black and white with very long tail; dark beak with broad pink patch. **Female:** short tail; brown back and wings; white head with dark cap and dark patch on the cheek.

F.

M.

Smew

F.

M.

Goosander

F.

M.

Ring-necked Duck

F.

M.

Scaup

F.

M.

Long-tailed Duck

Escape/Feral Ducks and Geese

Red-crested Pochard | *Netta rufina*
L 55cm WS 88cm

The male Red-crested Pochard is very colourful while the female has fairly plain plumage. It is native to an area around the Black Sea and central Asia. There are also small, scattered populations in Europe, which have expanded their breeding range during the 20th century. In Ireland, there was only a handful of records before 1950. Since then, records have increased with most seen in the east and north. Whether any of these are true wild birds is very difficult to prove because of the number of escaped birds present.

Chilöe Wigeon | *Anas sibilatrix*
L 48cm WS 80cm

The Chilöe Wigeon is native to southern South America and the Falkland Islands. (See Wigeon p. 45)

Ruddy Shelduck | *Tadorna ferruginea*
L 65cm WS 120cm

The Ruddy Shelduck is native to southern and eastern Europe, especially around the Black Sea and North Africa. In Ireland there have been a number of records of true wild birds in the past but with escaped birds breeding in the wild, all modern records are thought to refer to birds originating from captive origin.

Canada Goose | *Branta canadensis*
L 95cm WS 165cm

The Canada Goose is a native of North America. It migrates south to spend the winter further south in North America. In Ireland they were introduced in the early 19th century and it is suggested that there are now between 1,000–3,000 in the wild with most in the north, the highest concentrations being in Strangford Lough (Down) and the Erne catchment area (Fermanagh). It has been recorded breeding in many parts of Northern Ireland as well as The Lough in Cork city. There are fewer than 100 records of true wild Canada Geese in Ireland, usually seen with wild Greenland White-fronted or Barnacle Geese. (See Barnacle Goose p. 42, Brent Goose p.43)

Red-crested Pochard

F.

M.

Chiloe Wigeon

Ruddy Shelduck

Escape/Feral Ducks *(cont'd)*

Mandarin Duck | *Aix galericulata*
L 46cm   WS 70cm

Mandarin Duck is native to Eastern Russia, China, Japan and Korea. The male is brightly coloured while the female has fairly plain plumage. See female Wood Duck (below).

Wood Duck | *Aix sponsa*
L 50cm   WS 70cm

Also known as the Carolina Wood Duck, it is a native of North America. The male is very colourful while the female has fairly plain plumage. See female Mandarin Duck (above).

Ruddy Duck | *Oxyura jamaicensis*
L 40cm   WS 58cm

The Ruddy Duck gets its name from the male's bright ginger-red body plumage. Female has fairly plain plumage. Native of North and Central America and western South America. In Ireland it was first recorded breeding in the wild in 1973 and it is thought to have originated from the British population. Since then, the breeding population has increased slowly with most records from Lough Neagh. Ruddy Ducks have been seen in over 20 counties in Ireland but are nowhere common. Ruddy Duck has become a serious threat to the existence of the White-headed Duck in Europe because of its ability to hybridise with it.

F.

Mandarin Duck

Br. M.

F.

Wood Duck

Br. M.

Ad. NBr. M.

Br. M.

Ruddy Duck

Cormorant, Shag, Divers and Grebes

These birds have been grouped together here as many of them can look superficially similar, can all be found in the same or similar habitats, and all dive underwater to hunt for food.

Cormorants and Shags are fish-eaters and dive underwater to hunt for food using only their feet to propel them through the water. They sit low in the water and have a snake-like neck and head. The plumage is usually dark and iridescent, especially noticeable during the breeding season. They also have a habit of holding out their wings when ashore. It is thought that this is because they have poorly developed oil glands and so cannot waterproof their wings as well as other diving birds, such as ducks, and therefore need to dry them out when the feathers become waterlogged. It is also suggested they do this to aid digestion. Cormorants breed on offshore islands, sea cliffs and even on islands on freshwater lakes. Shags are mainly marine in nature and are rarely seen on freshwater.

Divers spend most of their time on the water and catch their food by diving underwater. They are able to stay underwater for long periods

Little Grebe

of time. In North America the collective name for these birds is 'loons'. This word is derived from either Old English or Scandinavian words meaning clumsy or awkward, a reference to the fact that on land they are not able to walk with ease. They very rarely breed in Ireland and are mainly winter visitors around our coast. Unlike the Cormorants and Shags, they usually slide underwater without a jump or splash. They normally spend the winter on salt water and breed on inland lakes. The largest of them, the Great Northern Diver, breeds in Iceland, Greenland and North America. The Red-throated Diver breeds here in very small numbers in the north of the island.

Grebes also hunt by diving underwater. They are more common than the Divers. They all breed on inland lakes, ponds and canals and are regularly seen on the coast in winter. They all have very short tails and legs set far back on the body and, like the Divers, do not move with ease when on land. Their feet are lobed instead of webbed and all will carry newly hatched chicks on their backs to keep them warm.

Cormorant | Broigheall | *Phalacrocorax carbo*
L 80–95cm WS 125–145cm AY CB Sea/Coast/Estuary/Wetland

Diving bird; bigger than Mallard; sexes similar; strong, grey, hook-tipped beak; large webbed feet; thick snake-like neck; swims low in water/slightly raised beak; jumps up and out as it dives. **Adult**: all black; breeding plumage, white 'diamond' on thigh; orange/white throat patch. **1ˢᵗW**: pale belly/throat. **In flight:** runs along water surface to take off; shallow, rapid wingbeats with intermittent glides; neck slightly bent; low over water or very high on its own or in group travelling in lines or Vs. Usually skis along water when landing. **Voice**: usually silent. (See Shag p. 69, Great Northern Diver p. 70, Black-throated Diver p. 74.)

Ad. Br.

Im.

chick

Ad. Br.

d. Br.

Ad. Br.

Im.

d. NBr.

Ad. Br.

Im.

Shag | Seaga | *Phalacrocorax aristotelis*
L 65–80cm   WS 90–105cm   AY   CB   Coast/Estuary

Diving bird; smaller, less robust version of the Cormorant; sexes similar; long, slim beak; short, stout, dark webbed feet; slim neck and head, more obvious forehead. **Br**: distinctive forward-curling dark crown tufts, all-dark iridescent plumage and thin yellow patch below the eye. **NBr**: loses its tufts and the yellow patch gets dull. **IstW**: unlike the Cormorant, is grey-brown rather than white/grey-white below. **In flight**: no obvious markings; direct flight, usually low over water; thin, straight neck. **Voice**: usually silent. (See Cormorant p. 68, Great Northern Diver p. 70, Red-throated Diver p. 71, Black-throated Diver p. 74.)

Ad. Br.

Ad. NBr.

Juv.

Great Northern Diver | Lóma mór | *Gavia immer*
L 76–84cm   WS 130–144cm   A/W/Sp   NB   Coast/Estuary

Cormorant-sized. Told from swimming Cormorant/Red-throated Diver by thicker beak held horizontally. **NBr**: dagger-shaped, light-grey beak, dark tip/culmen; noticeable forehead/flat crown; pale around eye; dark upperparts; white underside; indistinct dark half-collar; short tail. **Br**: black and white spotting on back; thin white stripes on side neck forming incomplete collar: **1ˢᵗ W**: pale-edged (scaly) back/wing feathers; looks paler than adult at distance. **In flight**: dark/unmarked upperparts, white underside; white underwing with dark trailing edge; looks dark-headed from distance; feet project well beyond short tail. **Voice:** usually silent outside breeding season. (See Cormorant p. 68, Shag p. 69, Red-throated Diver p. 71, Black-throated Diver p. 74)

NBr.

NBr.

Br.

NBr.

chick

Br.

Red-throated Diver | Lóma rua | *Gavia stellate*
L 58–64cm   WS 100–110cm   A/W/Sp   RB   Estuary/Coast

Mallard-sized; smaller than Great Northern Diver, p. 70; sexes similar; up-tilted, thin, dagger-shaped beak. **NBr**: pale-headed from distance; no obvious forehead; pale grey crown/nape, white in front of eye; cheeks/underside white; back/wings dark grey with pale flecks; no obvious tail. **Br**: red throat patch; grey face/side of neck; unpatterned dark grey-brown upperparts. **In flight**: direct flight; rapid wingbeats; dark/unmarked upperparts, white underside/white underwing with dark trailing edge. Legs project well beyond short tail. **Voice**: Usually silent; during breeding season, loud, eerie, plaintive song/calls. (See Great Northern Diver p. 70, Shag p. 69, Cormorant p. 68, Black-throated Diver p. 74.)

chick

Ad. Br.

courtship display

Ad. in moult

Ad. NBr.

Ad. N

Great Crested Grebe | Foitheach mór/Lúnadán | *Podiceps cristatus*
L 46–50cm   WS 60–70cm   A/W/Sp   SB   Wetland/Estuary

Smaller than Mallard; sexes similar; dives. **Br**: unmistakeable in breeding plumage; long, thin neck/striking head pattern with large chestnut/black tufts. **NBr**: straight, pink, dagger-shaped beak; thin, dark line between the eye and base of bill; dark crown; white face/neck/underside; dark grey-brown flanks. **Juv/1st W**: very young birds have black-and-white-striped head/neck; stripes disappear by early winter. **In flight**: looks long-bodied; large white patches on inner half of wings; very fast wingbeats; outstretched, slightly drooping neck; feet project beyond short tail. **Voice**: usually silent. Display call is a guttural *krraaa-krraaa*, also a higher *aaah-aaah*. (See Red-necked Grebe p.74)

Little Grebe | Spágaire tonn | *Tachybaptus ruficollis*
L 25–29cm WS 40–45cm AY CB Wetland/Estuary

Small diving bird, much smaller than Mallard; short, dark beak in Br plumage/ pale in NBr plumage with dark culmen; dark, lobed feet set far back on body. From a distance looks dark in colour; characteristic shape with a blunt fluffy rear end; buoyant appearance. **Br:** chestnut neck/ear coverts; creamy spot at base of short beak. **NBr:** pale throat; light brown neck/breast/flanks. **In flight:** all-dark upperparts. When disturbed will run along water surface with wings fluttering, into cover. Flight is fast/straight. **Voice:** call is a high, loud, long and whinnying trill. Chicks will often ride on the back of parent. (See Slavonian and Black-necked Grebe p. 74)

Scarce & Rare

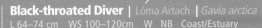

NBr.

Black-throated Diver | Lóma Artach | *Gavia arctica*
L 64–74 cm   WS 100–120cm   W   NB   Coast/Estuary

Smaller than Great Northern Diver, p. 70. **NBr**: dark grey crown and nape; sharp, straight division between grey nape and white throat; dark back; when on water there is a white patch at water level towards the tail; no white around eye; holds beak horizontally.

NBr.

Slavonian Grebe | Foitheach cluasach | *Podiceps auritus*
L 31–38cm   WS 52–62cm   W   NB   Estuary/Wetland

Small diving bird; larger than Little Grebe, p. 73. **NBr**: black and white; short beak, usually with pale tip; red eye; black cap and white cheeks; pale spot between eye and beak.

NBr.

Black-necked Grebe | Foitheach Píbdhubh | *Podiceps nigricollis*
L 28–38cm   WS 52–55cm   W   NB   Estuary/Wetland

Small diving bird; a little larger than Little Grebe, p. 73. **NBr**: similar to Slavonian Grebe; short, thin beak, red eye; black cap; white cheeks with dark grey behind the eye; more peaked crown. Darker-looking head and neck than Slavonian Grebe.

moulting

NBr.

Red-necked Grebe | Foitheach Píbrua | *Podiceps grisegena*
L 40–46cm   WS 78–84cm   W   NB   Estuary

A diving bird; bigger than Slavonian or Black-necked Grebe above but a bit smaller and thicker necked than Great Crested Grebe, p. 72. **NBr**: Straight dark dagger-shaped beak with variable amounts of yellow at the base; dark crown; pale chin and upper neck, dark front of neck; white wing patches visible in flight.

Note: Images not to scale

Auks

Puffin

Auks are represented by only a few species in Ireland, but they more than make up for this in numbers, especially in the breeding season when hundreds of thousands of them cram onto cliff ledges around the coast. They all hunt for fish and occasionally crustaceans by diving underwater and using their wings to 'fly' through the water in pursuit of prey. They only come to shore to breed. Some, like the Guillemot, lay their single egg on bare rock and pack tightly together on a cliff ledge. Others, like the well-known Puffin, breed in a burrow or under boulders. Long before they can fly, the chicks of the Razorbill jump from the cliff ledge where they were born and are fed by and swim after their father, sometimes for hundreds of kilometres, until they can fly and fend for themselves. All leave the breeding cliffs and spend the winter at sea. Though not closely related to penguins, because of their marine lifestyle they have come to resemble them in many ways. However, unlike penguins, they can fly. All have relatively short wings and usually fly close to the surface of the water with very rapid wingbeats. One member of this group, the Great Auk, which was once seen in Ireland, is now extinct. The last one to be seen alive in Ireland was captured off the Waterford coast in 1834.

bridled form

Ad. Br.

Ad. Br.

ch

Razorbill

Ad. Br.

Ad. NB

1st W.

Guillemot | Muiréan | *Uria aalga*
L 38–45cm   WS 64–73cm   AY   CB   Sea/Coast

Rook-sized; sexes similar; slim, dagger-shaped, all-dark beak; very short black legs set far back on body; webbed feet; dives to hunt. **Br:** head/upperparts chocolate-brown; white underside, white secondary stripe visible on closed wing. Some have white eye ring/line from rear of eye ('bridled' form). **NBr:** throat/side of face white; long, downcurving, narrow black stripe extends back from eye. **1ˢᵗ W:** shorter beak, less streaked flanks. **In flight:** direct/rapid wingbeats; chocolate-brown and white upperparts, sharp beak; feet projecting beyond tail. **Voice:** very noisy at breeding colonies; slightly muted, drawn-out *ooaarrrrr* easily heard above din of other breeding seabirds. (See Razorbill p. 77, Puffin p. 78, Little Auk p. 80.)

Ad. and chick

Ad. Br.

.d. W.
oulting

1st W.

Razorbill | Crosán | *Alca torda*
L 38–40cm   WS 64–68cm   AY   CB   Sea/Coast

Slightly smaller than Rook; sexes similar; dives to hunt. **Br**: stubby, stout black beak
with vertical white line; white line from the eye to the base of the top of the beak.
Black head, neck and upperparts; white secondary stripe visible on the closed wing;
white underside. **NBr**: throat and side of face white. **1ˢᵗ W**: beak slightly smaller with
no white on it. **In flight**: fast, direct flight; rapid wingbeats; black and white; blunt beak
and feet rarely projecting beyond the tail. (See Guillemot p. 76, Puffin p. 78, Little
Auk p. 80.)

Puffin | Puifín | *Fratercula arctica*
L 28–32cm   WS 53–59cm   Sp/Su/A   CB   Sea/Coast

Small auk, slightly smaller than a Jackdaw; sexes similar. **Br**: brightly coloured, large, triangular beak, obvious pale cheeks, black upperparts white underside; orange legs. **NBr**: duller, slightly thinner beak and sooty face. **I st W**: like NBr adult but with much smaller beak. **In flight**: black and white, fast with rapid wingbeats, slightly smaller and blunter-headed than Razorbill or Guillemot; pale cheeks obvious. **Voice**: makes a low moaning *aaawwwwrrrrr* sound in or near the nesting burrow. (See Razorbill p. 77, Guillemot p. 76, Little Auk p. 80.)

Ad. Br.

Ad. Br.

Ad. Br.

Ad. Br.

Ad. NBr.

1st Y.

Ad. Br. diving

Black Guillemot | Foracha dhubh | *Cepphus grylle*
L 31–35cm   WS 54–56cm   AY   CB   Sea/Coast/Estuary

Size of a Jackdaw; sexes similar; sits low on the water. **Br**: all dark with large, oval, white wing patches, bright red legs, short, pointed beak, red gape; white lining to the underwing. Birds in their first summer look almost entirely black with small patches of white on the wing. **NBr**: head and back looks pale, white wing patches, dark flecked on 1ˢᵗ W birds. **In flight**: direct flight; rapid wingbeats, usually low over the water; white wing patches very obvious and also white rump in winter.

Scarce & Rare

W.

Little Auk | *Alle alle*
L 20cm WS 34–37cm W NB Sea/Coast

As name suggests, much smaller than other auks. Adult **NBr**: stubby, black beak; black upperparts and white underside with white-edged scapulars looking like white lines on the closed wing. **Br**: head and neck black. Very young razorbills can look similar but do not have white-edged scapulars. Rapid, buzzing, direct flight. (See Puffin p. 78, Guillemot p. 76, Razorbill p. 77)

W.

W.

Note: Images not to scale

Seabirds (Fulmar, Shearwaters, Petrels and Gannet)

Fulmar, Petrels and Shearwaters spend most of their time on the open sea. Collectively known as 'tubenoses', they have specially modified beaks with an external tube or tubes linked to the nasal passages to improve their sense of smell, which they use to locate food and their breeding colony, and also salt glands for the excretion of excess salt through the tube or tubes. The Fulmar is the most familiar as it nests on sea cliff ledges

Storm Petrel

all around the coast and it is hard to believe that it was only confirmed as breeding for the first time in Ireland in 1911. Also in this group are Petrels and Shearwaters, which nest in burrows on remote islands, coming ashore only at night to avoid predators. They have poorly developed leg muscles for walking and are therefore vulnerable to attack on land.

Ireland is a very important breeding location for this group of birds. They are expert fliers, especially in strong winds. The Petrels get their name from way they patter and run across the surface of the water when feeding and look like they are walking on water, which relates to the bible story about Saint Peter trying to walk on water. All are related to the Albatrosses and, despite their harsh environment, are long lived with some like the Manx Shearwater living over 50 years. The ocean is their home and many travel thousands of miles each year. Manx Shearwaters winter off the west coast of South America and our smallest seabird, the Storm Petrel, has been found wintering off South Africa.

The Gannet is the only species of the gannet family represented in Ireland. They feed on fish, which they catch by diving into the sea, often from great heights and descend underwater up to 25 metres. They usually swallow their catch underwater to avoid it being stolen when they surface. They are closely related to the Cormorant and exotic species like the boobies and noddies. Ireland is one of the most important breeding places for the Gannet in Europe. The BirdWatch Ireland reserve at Little Skellig in Kerry holds over 25,000 breeding pairs each summer.

Manx Shearwater | Cánóg dhubh | *Puffinus puffinus*
L 33–35cm WS 78–82cm Sp/Su/A CB Sea/Coast

A bit smaller than a Rook; sexes similar; black upperparts and white underside. **In flight**: stiff wingbeats; glides on slightly bowed narrow wings, arching glides in windy conditions. Often seen feeding with Gannets and Kittiwake, forming large flocks on the water called rafts. Will dive at a shallow angle from just above the surface when hunting. Not usually seen close to land. (See Balearic Shearwater p. 86, Great Shearwater p. 86, Cory's Shearwater p. 86, Sooty Shearwater p. 86)

Storm Petrel | Guairdeall | *Hydrobates pelagicus*
L 16cm WS 38–40cm CB Sea

Smallest European seabird; size of a Swallow; rarely seen close to shore or resting on water; sexes similar. **Adult**: at a distance, all-dark upperparts and white rump patch; long wings; distinct white bar on the underwing; square-ended dark tail; white on rump extends onto the side of the undertail. **1ˢᵗ W**: in first autumn some have a thin, short, pale stripe on ther upperwing. **In flight**: flutters puppet-like with legs pattering and running on the surface when hunting, erratic flight. (See Leach's Storm Petrel p. 86.)

Gannet | Gainéad/Ogastún | *Morus bassanus*
L 92–96cm   WS 170–180cm   Sp/Su/A   B   Sea/Coast

Our largest seabird; plunge-dives from a height with sweptback wings when hunting.
Adult: unmistakeable; brilliant white plumage, long wings, black wing tips; pointed tail;
head yellow, though not always noticeable at a distance; large, conical beak. **Juv/Im**:
dark brown with pale spots and streaks, gradually becoming whiter as it reaches
adulthood, usually taking four to six years. **In flight**: when not feeding, gannets often
fly in V-formation or in single file just above the waves. Glides and soars in strong
wind. **Voice**: at the breeding colony, a rapidly repeated guttural *dirraaw-dirraaw-
dirraaw*, varying slightly in pitch, forming a continuous chorus.

'Blue Fulmar'

Fulmar | Fulmaire | *Fulmarus glacialis*
L 46–50cm WS 105–110cm AY CB Sea/Coast

Bigger than a Rook; sexes similar. **All ages:** white head; thick-necked; blue-grey or brown-grey upperparts, white underside; light grey tail; short stout 'tubenose' beak. Darker, higher-latitude birds are called 'Blue Fulmar'. **In flight:** pale patches at base of primaries. Shallow, stiff wingbeats punctuated with glides. The stronger the wind the longer and more undulating the glides, and like its relative, the albatross, it glides effortlessly even in gale-force winds; stout cigar-shaped body. **Voice:** usually vocal only at the nest, where it makes a laughing, squawking chatter.

Scarce & Rare

Cory's Shearwater | Cánóg Cory | *Calonectris diomedea*
L 50–55cm   WS 120–125cm   A   NB   Sea

Fulmar-sized; larger than Manx Shearwater, p. 82. **All ages**: grey-brown head; thick yellow beak, dark tip; grey-brown back, rump and dark tail; dark brown wings above and white below with dark trailing edge to the wing; glides on long bowed wings.

Great Shearwater | Cánóg mhór | *Puffinus gravis*
L 44–50cm   WS 106–120cm   A   NB   Sea

Larger than Manx Shearwater, p. 82. **All ages**: similar to Cory's Shearwater but dark cap and almost complete white collar; usually has white crescent on the rump; white underside with brown smudging on the belly; dark beak; can look like a small, young Gannet at a distance.

Sooty Shearwater | Cánóg dhorcha | *Puffinus griseus*
L 40–50cm   WS 94–105cm   A   NB   Sea

A bit bigger than Manx Shearwater, p. 82. **All ages**: as name suggests, looks all-dark sooty brown; usually fairly rapid, stiff wingbeats, also glides; narrow, long and pointed wing shape; underwing coverts silvery-white and flash when catching sunlight.

Leach's Storm Petrel | Guairdeall gabhlach | *Oceanodroma leucorhoa*
L 18–20cm   WS 44–48cm   A   RB   Sea

Similar to but slightly bigger than European Storm Petrel, p. 83. **All ages**: forked tail; no white on the underwing; dark primaries and secondaries contrast with paler secondary coverts forming a pale wing panel above; very erratic flight.

Balearic Shearwater | Cánóg Bhailéarach | *Puffinus mauretanicus*
L 34–38cm   WS 80–90cm   Sp/A   NB   Sea

Marginally bigger than Manx Shearwater, p. 82. **All ages**: looks similar but browner upperparts and dusky below, especially around the head, neck and base of the underwing. Rarely as dark as Sooty Shearwater. Unlike Manx Shearwater, feet project a little beyond the tail, only visible at close range.

Cory's Shearwater

Great Shearwater

Sooty Shearwater

Leach's Storm Petrel

Balearic Shearwater

Note: Images not to scale

Gulls, Terns and Skuas

Gulls are found everywhere in Ireland, from the inland-nesting Black-headed Gull to the Great Black-backed Gull found breeding mainly on cliffs and offshore islands. They have adapted to living with humans. Two examples of this are the noisy clouds of scavenging gulls following a trawler into port and the trail of gulls following the plough in search of insects and worms.

Roseate Tern

Terns come here in their thousands each summer from their wintering grounds in Africa and beyond. The Roseate Tern, which is the rarest breeding tern in Europe, has one of its largest colonies on the BirdWatch Ireland/DOE-managed island of Rockabill off the north Dublin coast.

Skuas are mainly non-breeding summer visitors and are often referred to as sea-hawks or pirates. They chase other seabirds, usually gulls and terns, until they surrender the food they are carrying.

Juv.

3rd W.

Ad.

Ad.

chick

Ad.

2nd W.

Juv./1st W.

2nd

Great Black-backed Gull | Droimneach mór | *Larus marinus*
L 69–73cm WS 156–160cm AY CB Coast/Estuary

Largest Irish gull, much bigger than Black-headed Gull. **Adult**: black back/wings; white wing tips; flesh-pink legs; heavy yellow beak with red spot. **Juv/Im**: plumage initially a complex pattern of black/brown/white showing more contrast than on other young large gulls. As it matures, back turns black first ('saddle-back' appearance). **In flight**: black back; broad black wings with a white trailing/leading edge; white wing tips; strong agile flight. Young birds: pale inner primaries/indistinct dark tail band visible in flight. **Voice**: deep calls, including a short *ouawk*. (See Lesser Black-backed Gull p. 91, Young Gulls p. 108)

Ad. Br.

Ad. Br.

2nd S.

2nd S.

1st S.

Juv.

Juv.

Juv.

Ad.

Juv.

Lesser Black-backed Gull | Droimneach | *Larus fuscus*
L 50–58cm   WS 120–140cm   AY   CB   Coast/Estuary

Noticeably smaller than Great Black-backed Gull. **Adult**: dark grey back/wings with white wing tips; yellow-ochre legs; yellow beak with red spot. **Juv/Im**: starts out with complex patterns of black/brown/white; looks darker overall than other young gulls; all dark primaries/secondaries; pink legs/dark beak on young birds; gradually reaches adult plumage after four years. **In flight**: dark grey back/wings, white trailing edge with black on outer primaries with white wing tips; solid dark tail band on younger birds. (See Great Black-backed Gull p. 90, Young Gulls p. 108.)

1st W.

3rd Yr.

2nd Yr.

Ad. W.

3rd Yr.

Ad. Br.

2nd Yr.

Ad. Br.

chick

1st W.

3rd W.

3rd W.

Herring Gull | Faoileán scadán | *Larus argentatus*
L 55–67cm WS 130–158cm AY CB Sea/Coast/Estuary

Bigger than Black-headed Gull. **Adult**: pale grey back/wings; black-and-white wing tips; pink legs; stout yellow beak/red spot; yellow iris. **NBr**: head/neck mottled grey-brown. **Juv/Im**: complex patterns of black/brown/white; dark outer primaries; initially black beak/dark iris/black tail band. Grey-backed in 2nd W; adult plumage in fourth year. **In flight**: light blue-grey back/upper wings; black-and-white wing tips, thin white trailing edge. Im: pale inner primaries/solid dark tail band; varying amounts of brown on body/wings, dark wing tips on 1st Y. **Voice**: includes loud, repeated *kuwaa*/laugh-like *agah-ga-ga*. (See Common Gull p. 93, Young Gulls p. 108, Yellow-legged Gull p. 104.)

Common Gull | Faoileán bán | *Larus canus*
L 40–42cm WS 110–120cm Sp/A/W SB Estuary/Wetland

Black-headed Gull sized. **Adult**: grey back/wings with white trailing edge, black wing tips with large white spots; dull yellow beak; legs yellow-green to grey. **NBr**: streaking on head; beak grey at base with some black near tip. **Juv/Im**: adult plumage in three years. 1st Y: grey back; no obvious white on wings; white tail; black tail band; black-tipped pink bill, grey-pink legs. 2nd Y like non-breeding adult; less white/more black on wing tips; thicker black band on beak. **In flight**: noticeable white wing tips on adult. **Voice**: very squeaky. (See Ring-billed Gull p. 104, Herring Gull p. 92, Kittiwake p. 98, Young Gulls p. 108.)

Ad. NBr.

Ad. Br.

Ad. NBr.

Ad.

1st W.

1st W.

1st W.

Juv.

Ad. NBr.

Black-headed Gull | Faoileán an chaipín | *Chroicocephalus ridibundus*
L 38–44cm WS 94–105cm AY CB Sea/Coast/Estuary/Wetland/Farmland

Jackdaw-sized. **Adult Br**: dark chocolate-brown head; white underside; pale grey
back/wings; dark red beak/legs. **Adult NBr**: dark spot behind eye; two dark smudge-
lines on head; legs/base of beak paler. **1st Y**: dark brown/black on wings; thin black
tail band; orange-yellow legs; pale brown-yellow beak/black tip. **In flight**: adult:
pale grey back/wings; white leading edge to outer primaries forming white
triangle (above and below) with black trailing edge. 1st Y: reduced white on outer
primaries; dark trailing edge to secondaries; brown wing coverts; black tail band.
Voice: noisy, high-pitched call; includes thin-sounding, drawn-out *kaaww*; also
softer chatter. (See Mediterranean Gull p. 95, Little Gull p. 104, Young Gulls p. 108.)

v./1st W.

d. NBr.

d. S.

st W.

Juv.

1st S. moulting
to 2nd W.

2nd W.

Ad. NBr.

Ad. Br.

2nd W.

Ad. NBr.

Mediterranean Gull | Sléibhín Meánmhuirí | *Larus melanocephalus*
L 37–39cm   WS 94–98cm   All Year   RB   Estuary

Black-headed Gull sized. **Adult Br**: jet-black hood, broken white eye ring; pale grey back/wings, white towards tips; no black body plumage; stout red beak with yellow tip; long red legs. **Adult NBr**: variable dark streaks from behind eye across top of head. **Juv/Im**: more black/grey than young Black-headed Gulls. 1st W: dark legs/beak; thin black tail band. 2nd Y: looks like adult, has thin black markings on white primaries. **In flight**: adults have no black on wings; 2nd Y has thin black lines on primaries; 1st W looks black, white and grey. (See Black-headed Gull p. 94, Little Gull p. 104, Young Gulls p. 108.)

1st W.

2nd W.

Ad

Ad.

2nd W.

Ac

3rd W.

2nd W.

2nd W.

2nd W.

1st W.
(faded)

1st W.

Glaucous Gull | Faoileán glas | *Larus hyperboreus*
L 63–67cm WS 154–158cm A/W/Sp NB Coast/Estuary

Great Black-backed Gull sized; heavy build; no black on wing tips. **Adult:** white wing tips; NBr: can be heavily streaked brown on head/neck//breast; stout yellow beak with red spot; pink legs. Wings typically project *just beyond* tail. **Juv/Im:** start off brown on body; wings finely marked/wing tips are pale; gradually changing to adult plumage over four years, can look almost all white in 2nd/3rd Y. Beak pink base/ black tip. **In flight:** pale wing tips on young birds; overall pale gull in and as it nears adult plumage. From below, paler primaries/secondaries stand out against rest of underwing. (See Iceland Gull p. 97, Herring Gull p. 92, Young Gulls p. 108.)

Iceland Gull | Faoileán Íoslannach | *Larus glaucoides*
L 54–58cm WS 138–142cm A/W/Sp NB Coast/Estuary

Bigger than Black-headed Gull; very similar to but smaller than Glaucous Gull (p. 96.); no black wing tips. **Adult**: white wing tips usually project _well beyond_ tail. NBr: brown streaking on head/nape/side of neck; greenish-yellow beak with small red spot. **Juv/Im**: brown body; wings finely marked; pale wing tips; adult plumage in four years; can look almost all white in 2nd/3rd year. Beak dark with red tint towards the base; gets paler with age but not always bicoloured as Glaucous Gull. **In flight**: pale-winged gull. From below, paler primaries/secondaries stand out against rest of underwing. (See Glaucous Gull p. 96, Herring Gull p. 92, Young Gulls p. 108.)

1st S.

Ad. N[

1st W.

Ad. Br.

Ad. B

Ad. Br.

Ad. B

Ad. NBr.

1st W.

Juv.

Ad. Br.

Ad. NBr.

Kittiwake | Saidhbhéar | *Rissa tridactyla*
L 37–41cm WS 104–108cm AY CB Sea/Coast

Black-headed Gull sized. **Adult**: yellow beak; dark eye; short dark legs; grey back/wings; black wing tips. NBr: grey nape/dark smudge behind eye. **Juv/Im**: black half collar at base of neck, fades in 1ˢᵗ Y; black smudge behind eye; black beak, turns yellow with age; some black on wings; black-tipped tail. Reaches adult plumage after three years. **In flight**: adult has grey back/inner wing, paler towards primaries/'dipped in ink' black tips; Juv/Im: black 'M' pattern on wings; buoyant agile flight. **Voice**: a loud sound like 'kittiwaakke', often repeated. Usually silent outside breeding season. (See Common Gull p. 93, Sabine's Gull p. 104, Little Gull p. 104, Young Gulls p. 108.)

st W.

Ad. NBr.

Ad. Br.

Ad. Br.

Juv.

Ad. NBr.

Ad. NBr.

colony

Sandwich Tern | Geabhróg scothdhubh | *Sterna sandvicensis*
L 38–42cm WS 100cm Sp/Su/A CB Coast/Estuary

About the size of Black-headed Gull; long, dark beak with pale yellow tip, short black legs. **Br**: black crown and nape, shaggy crest usually only visible when on the ground, forked tail. **NBr**: pale forehead and front half of the crown. **Juv/Im**: no yellow tip to the beak; varying amounts of dark-tipped and dark-edged feathers on the wings and back. **In flight**: when hunting, flies with beak pointing down; large, pale-looking tern with dark grey outer primaries. **Voice**: distinctive, loud, high-pitched, grating call. (See Common Tern p. 100, Arctic Tern p. 101, Roseate Tern p. 106.)

Juv.

Ad.

Juv.

Ad. Br.

chick

Juv.

Common Tern | Geabhróg | *Sterna hirundo*
L 31–35cm WS 82–95cm Sp/Su/A CB Sea/Coast/Estuary

Smaller than Black-headed Gull; plunge-dives. **Br**: dark-tipped red beak; black crown/ nape; long, slim, pointed wings, dark grey on outer primaries; long, deeply forked tail; short red legs. Wing tips _usually project beyond the tip_ of tail. **NBr**: white forehead, black beak. **Juv/Im**: variable amounts of ginger-brown on back/wings; plain grey primaries; dark secondary bar; pale forehead; darker beak with orange base. **In flight**: from below translucent trailing edge to inner primaries. **Voice**: very vocal at breeding colony; loud, high-pitched, screeching calls. (See Arctic Tern p. 101, Roseate Tern p. 106.)

Ad. Br.

Juv.

Ad. Br.

1st S.

Juv.

chick

Arctic Tern | Geabhróg Artach | *Sterna paradisaea*
L 33–37cm WS 66–80cm Sp/Su/A CB Sea/Coast/Estuary

Smaller/slimmer than Black-headed Gull; very similar to Common Tern, p. 100.
Br: dark red beak; black crown/nape; deeply forked tail; very short red legs. Pale
grey back/wings, darker on primaries. Wing tips *do not usually project beyond the tip*
of tail. **NBr**: dark brown beak; white forehead. **Juv/Im**: variable amounts of black/
ginger-brown tips to back/wing feathers; no dark secondary bar; dark primary tips. **In
flight**: from below, all primaries pale with thin black bar along trailing edge of outer
primaries; looks pale overall, black cap, deeply forked tail. **Voice**: very vocal around
breeding colony with harsh high-pitched calls. (See Common Tern p. 100, Roseate

Ad. light phas[e]

Ad.
dark phase

Juv.

Central
tail feathers
missing

Ad.
dark phase

Ad. light phase

Ad. light phase

Ad. dark phase

Arctic Skua | Meirleach Artach | *Stercorarius parasiticus*
L 38–44cm   WS 110–118cm   Sp/Su/A   NB   Sea/Coast

Tern p. 106.)

Black-headed Gull sized; stout dark beak; white wing flashes; dark legs; straight, pointed central tail feathers. Two colour forms: **Adult Pale** – pale yellow collar; dark cap; pale feathers at base of beak; white breast/belly; grey breast sides, can form breast band. **Adult Dark** – dark brown plumage with white wing flashes. **Juv/Im**: vary from all dark to tan with dark barring on belly. **In flight**: wing flashes more prominent on underwing; pointed central tail feathers, can break off or be very short. Very agile, chases seabirds to force them to surrender food. (See Great Skua p. 103, Pomarine

Great Skua | Meirleach mór | *Stercorarius skua*
L 54–58cm   WS 132–140cm   Sp/Su/A   RB   Sea/Coast

Skua p. 106, Long-tailed Skua p. 106.)
Smaller than Great Black-backed Gull. **Adult**: unmistakeable; looks like a large, stocky, dark brown gull with noticeable white wing flashes and no projecting central tail feathers. Some birds can look paler brown on the body. **Juv/Im**: darker than adult; smooth, unstreaked underside; smaller wing flashes. **In flight**: white wing flashes, obvious from above and below, stocky build, gull-like flight. Like all skuas will chase other seabirds to force them to surrender their catch. Will swoop repeatedly on intruders when nesting. **Voice**: usually silent. (See dark forms of Arctic Skua p. 102,

Scarce & Rare

Ring-billed Gull | Faoileán bandghobach | *Larus delawarensis*
L 42–49cm   WS 114–123cm   W   NB   Estuary/Coast

Similar size and appearance to Common Gull, p. 93. **All ages**: paler grey back, same grey as Black-headed Gull. **Juv/Im**: thicker beak usually pink with black tip. **2nd W** and **adult**: no obvious white trailing edge to the wings; no obvious white crescent on the closed wing just behind the primaries. Adult beak yellow with a black band and paler yellow tip and yellow iris.

Sabine's Gull | Sléibhín Sabine | *Xema sabini*
L 30–36cm   WS 80–86cm   A   NB   Sea/Coast

Superficially resembles Kittiwake, p. 98, slightly smaller. **Adult**: like Juv/Im Kittiwake but no black on inner wing and all white, more deeply forked tail; dark beak with yellow tip, grey-black head in Br plumage. **Juv/Im**: similar to Juv/Im Kittiwake but dark brown on back, inner wing and on head.

Little Gull | Sléibhín beag | *Hydrocoloeus minutus*
L 24–28cm   WS 62–68cm   A/W   NB   Coast/Estuary

Smallest gull, noticeably smaller than Black-headed Gull, p. 94; fluttering tern-like flight. **Adult**: from above, pale grey back and wings with thin white trailing edge and white wing tips. Almost black underwing with thin white trailing edge. Black head and beak in Br plumage; dark spot behind eye and dark at rear of crown in NBr plumage. **Juv/Im**: thin black beak; from above, black, grey and white back and wings; grey-pink legs. Back pale grey on 1st W and variable black lines on outer primaries in 2nd Y. (See young Kittiwake p. 98, Mediterranean Gull p. 95.)

Yellow-legged Gull | Faoileán cosa buí | *Larus michahellis*
L 52–58cm   WS 120–140cm   W   NB   Estuary/Coast

Adult: very similar to Herring Gull, p. 92 but has yellow instead of pink legs. Slightly darker grey on the back and wings. **Juv/Im**: younger bird look more like young Lesser Black-backed Gull p. 91 but tends to have a white head.

Ring-billed Gull (Ad.)

Sabine's Gull (Ad.)

Little Gull (Ad.)

Little Gull (1st W.)

Yellow-legged Gull (Ad.)

Note: Images not to scale

Scarce & Rare *(cont'd)*

Little Tern | Geabhróg bheag | *Sternula albifrons*
L 20–25cm   WS 40–46cm   S/A   RB   Coast/Sea

Much smaller than Common Tern, p. 100. **Adult Br**: thin, sharp, yellow beak with black tip; black cap and nape with triangular white forehead patch. **Adult NBr**: all-dark beak, white on forehead extends onto the crown. Juv/Im: black edges to grey back feathers; pale yellow-grey legs.

Black Tern | Geabhróg dhubh | *Chlidonias niger*
L 23–26cm   WS 56–61cm   W   NB   Estuary/Coast

Smaller than Common Tern, p. 100. **Adult Br**: grey wings, back and tail; black head, breast and belly; black beak; slightly forked tail. **NBr**: dark smudge on side of breast; black cap extending down behind the eye; rest of head, breast and belly white. **Juv/Im**: dark wings and back.

Roseate Tern | Geabhróg rósach | *Sterna dougallii*
L 33–36cm   WS 68–75cm   Su/A   RB   Sea/Coast

Very similar in size and colour to Common Tern, p. 100. **Adult Br**: very pale back and wings; thin, sharp black beak with red only at the base, all dark early in breeding season; pale rosy-pink wash on the breast and belly; no dark trailing edge on outer primaries. **Adult NBr**: white forehead, all-dark beak. **Juv/Im**: very scaly back and white secondaries; black short legs.

Pomarine Skua | Meirleach pomairineach | *Stercorarius pomarinus*
L 42–50cm   WS 115–125cm   A   NB   Sea/Coast

Smaller than Great Skua, p. 103; bigger and heavier build than Arctic Skua, p. 102. Like Arctic Skua, it occurs in pale and dark forms. Adult Br: elongated teardrop-shaped central tail feathers; pale form has no white on forehead and chin and usually has distinct dark breast band. Juv/Im: colder, darker plumage.

Long-tailed Skua | Meirleach earrfhada | *Stercorarius longicaudus*
L 35–40cm   WS 105–110cm   Sp/A   NB   Sea/Coast

Smaller and slimmer than Arctic Skua, p. 102. **Adult Br**: very long, thin central tail feathers; paler grey-brown on back and secondary coverts; wing flashes very faint. **Juv/Im**: very faint wing flashes; colder colours and scaly pattern on back and wing coverts.

Little Tern

Little Tern

Black Tern

Black Tern

Roseate Tern

Roseate Tern

Long-tailed Skua

narine Skua

Note: Images not to scale

Young Gulls

Common Gull

Kittiwake

Mediterranean
Gull

Black-headed Gull

Lesser Black-backed
Gull

Great Black-backed
Gull

Herring Gull

1st W. 'Kumlien's'
Iceland Gull

Iceland Gull

Glaucous Gull

Note: Images not to scale

Pomarine Skua p. 106, young gulls p. 108)

Grey Heron

Herons, Egrets and Crane

Herons and egrets have powerful beaks and long legs. They catch their prey in shallow water or on land by using their long necks to strike with great speed. Their diet is quite varied and includes fish, frogs and even rats and young birds. They usually nest in groups in trees, called heronries. Despite their large size they can be very susceptible to cold weather, when they find it difficult to catch food. The Grey Heron is the only common representative of this group in Ireland. Little Egrets, once shot for their brilliant white plumage and only occasional visitors to our shores 40 years ago, are now breeding here in increasing numbers. The Bittern, or *an Bonnán buí*, also a member of this group, was once a common breeding bird in Ireland. It became extinct here in the middle of the 19th century and now appears here only as a rare migrant.

Crane is included here mainly because people sometimes use the name Crane for the Grey Heron which superficially resembles this very elegant bird. They engage in very elaborate courtship 'dances' and are rarely seen alone. Unlike the herons and egrets they fly with their necks outstretched. They have a varied diet and they breed in northeastern Europe and winter around the Mediterranean.

Grey Heron | Corr éisc | *Ardea cinerea*
L 90–96cm WS 150–173cm AY CB Wetland/Estuary

Our tallest bird; large dagger-shaped beak. **Adult**: pale grey head; thick black stripe from eye to back of head; long neck; grey body; long legs. **Br**: long, thin feathers on neck/breast; two long black feathers from back of head; beak changes colour from dull yellow-orange to bright pink (NBr to Br). **Im**: greyer plumage, duller beak. **In flight**: bowed wings, slow wingbeats; neck tucked in/legs trailing beyond short tail. Wings/back grey with darker primaries/secondaries. Young birds not as clearly marked. **Voice**: loud *fraank* call. Sounds of adults/young at nest, day/night, are like a fairy-tale monster or someone getting sick! (See Crane p. 112.)

Little Egret | Éigrit bheag | *Egretta garzetta*
L 60–65cm WS 90–95cm AY SB Estuary/Wetland

Smaller and slimmer than the much larger Grey Heron and a bit bigger than a Curlew; sexes similar. **All ages:** yellow feet; long, thin, dark, dagger-shaped beak; all-white plumage. **Br:** develops long, thin, white feathers from the back of the head and lace-like feathers on the breast and back. **In flight:** flies slowly with bowed wings with neck tucked up and yellow feet visible on dark legs trailing beyond its short tail. **Voice:** usually silent but will make squawking noises when fighting or at the nest. (See Cattle Egret p. 114, Spoonbill p. 112.)

Scarce & Rare

Spoonbill | Leitheadach | *Platalea leucorodia*
L 80–90cm   WS 125–135cm   A/W/Sp   NB   Estuary/Wetland

Bigger than Little Egret (p. 111) and just a little bit smaller than Grey Heron p. 110; mainly all-white plumage; long beak with a spoon-like end; flies with neck outstretched. **Adult**: dark beak with yellow tip; long, shaggy crest and buff on breast in breeding plumage. **Juv/Im**: black tips to primaries, pale beak.

Bittern | Bonnán buí | *Botaurus stellaris*
L 70–80cm   WS 100–130cm   A/W   NB (formerly bred)   Wetland

Stocky and heron-like; a bit smaller than Grey Heron, p. 110. **All ages**: mottled and flecked black, browns, buff; stout, dagger-shaped yellow beak; relatively short pale legs. No noticeable markings. In flight: more hurried flight than Grey Heron. **Voice**: male song called 'booming', a low-pitched sound, which is a bit like the sound made by blowing into/across the opening of a large, empty bottle.

Crane | Corr | *Grus grus*
L 95–120cm   WS 180–220cm   A/W/Sp   NB (formerly bred)   Farmland/Wetland

A tall elegant bird which superficially resembles Grey Heron, p. 110. Flies with neck outstretched. **Adult**: largely grey with a black-and-white head and a red cap. Long 'untidy' black and grey tertials forming a rough tail. **Juv**: brown on the head and neck. **Voice:** loud, harsh, guttural sounds.

Spoonbill (Juv.)

Spoonbill (Ad.)

Bittern

Bittern

Crane (Ad.)

Ad.

Juv.

Ad.

Crane

Great White Egret

NBr.

Cattle Egret

Br.
Cattle Egret

Great White Egret | Éigrit mhór | *Ardea alba*
L 85–100cm   WS 148–168cm   AY   NB   Wetland/Estuary

Only slightly smaller than Grey Heron (p. 110) and much bigger than Little Egret (p. 111) and Cattle Egret (above). Long neck with obvious kink, beak yellow during NBr and dark during Br season, feet always dark and legs project well beyond the short tail in flight.

Cattle Egret | Éigrit eallaigh | *Bubulcus ibis*
L 46–52cm   WS 82–94cm   A/W/Sp   NB   Farmland

Superficially like Little Egret (p. 111) but has shorter, thicker neck; short, stout, yellow-orange, dagger-shaped beak, pink base in breeding season; all-white plumage with pale brown on head, breast and back in breeding season; pale iris; as name suggests seen more often in fields near livestock.

Note: Images not to scale

Moorhen

Rails and Crakes

Most members of this group live in or near wet areas with tall, dense vegetation. The Corncrake have, once very common all over Ireland, is now on the brink of extinction here . BirdWatch Ireland and the Royal Society for the Protection of Birds (RSPB), with co-operation from the wildlife service in the Department the Environment (DOE) and the international bird conservation organisation Birdlife International, are attempting to save this species from extinction in Ireland through land purchase and management and by advocating Corncrake-friendly farming practices.

chick (young)

Ad.

chick (old

Coot | Cearc cheannann | *Fulica atra*
L 36–40cm WS 70–80cm AY CB Wetland

Smaller than Mallard; dives; sexes similar. **Adult**: conspicuous white beak and forehead shield; black plumage; dark red eye; large, lobed green-grey feet. **Juv/Im**: paler than adults, especially on the head, neck and breast. Similar to young Moorhen (p. 117) but lacks white on the undertail; downy chicks dark brown with an orange-red head. **In flight**: all dark with narrow, white trailing edge to the secondaries. **Voice**: sounds include a loud short *krouw*, repeated mechanically, with several intermittent brief high-pitched nasal whistles. (See Moorhen p. 117.)

Ad.

Ad.

Juv.

m.

chick

Ad.

Ad.

Im.

Moorhen | Cearc uisce | *Gallinula chloropus*
L 32–35cm WS 50–55cm AY CB Wetland

Smaller than Mallard; sexes similar. **Adult**: bright red forehead shield; red/yellow beak; dark plumage, apart from some white streaks on flanks and two white patches on undertail; stout legs; large, lobed feet. **Juv/Im**: browner and paler; dull olive-yellow beak; downy young are all black with red/yellow beak. **In flight**: rarely seen in flight; when frightened or in danger, runs along water surface with neck outstretched and wings flapping furiously, making for the nearest cover of reeds or other waterside vegetation. **Voice**: makes many sounds. Usually a loud, harsh *krrrek* or a fast double-noted *ka-kik*. (See Coot p. 116, Water Rail p. 118.)

Water Rail | Ralóg uisce/Traonach uisce | *Rallus aquaticus*
L 22–26cm WS 38–45cm AY CB Wetland

Slightly smaller than Blackbird; dark red eye; long, thin, slightly downcurved pink-red beak, dark culmen and tip; long legs; large, unwebbed, pale pink feet. **Adult**: upperparts streaked black; brown back/wings; underside dark; grey face/neck/breast; belly/flanks heavily barred black/white; vent buff; undertail coverts white. **Juv/Im**: similar to adult but paler face/breast/belly; shorter dull beak. **In flight**: no obvious markings; legs hang down; usually only flies a short distance if disturbed. **Voice**: the easiest way to identify this secretive bird; loud grunting/squealing pig-like call from a reed bed or other waterside vegetation, mainly at dawn/dusk and at night. (See Moorhen p. 117, Corncrake p. 119.)

Corncrake | Traonach | *Crex crex*
L 22–26cm WS 46–53cm Su/A RB Farmland

Might be confused with a female Pheasant (p. 165) in long grass. **Adult:** size of a blackbird; heavy looking; pale grey face, throat and breast; brown flanks with indistinct pale stripes. **In flight:** chestnut-brown wings; trailing legs. **Unique call:** loud rasping *crex crex*, like drawing a fingernail quickly across a toothed comb. Regularly calls at night. (See Water Rail p. 118, Grey Partridge p. 167, Quail p. 167.)

Waders

After perching birds, this is the largest and one of the most important groups of birds in Ireland. It includes waders such as the Oystercatcher, Plovers, Snipe and Sandpipers. Every winter our coasts, estuaries and wetlands become the feeding grounds for hundreds of thousands of waders. During the short winter days they spend most of their time on mud, sand or wet grassland

Redshank

feeding on a variety of small creatures that live on or near the surface. Some feed almost 24 hours a day; stopping only when the tide covers their feeding grounds. They normally feed in flocks ranging from just a few birds to thousands. When a large flock of waders, such as Dunlin or Golden Plover, takes to the sky, they fly over the estuary as a unit, turning and twisting in unison. They will bank from side to side, flashing their pale undersides, beginning at the front of the flock and spreading along its length. This movement is called 'wheeling', and provides a kind of natural firework display, difficult to surpass.

The birds' bills have developed in various ways to exploit the different types of prey on which they feed, thus avoiding competition for the same food source on the same mudflat or sandbar. Some, such as the Plovers, feed by sight and have very short beaks, while others like the Dunlin use their sense of touch to find their prey below the surface, usually with long, thin and often curved beaks.

Ireland is internationally important for waders, with large numbers coming here each winter from their breeding grounds in Arctic North America right through to Northern Europe and across Siberia. Only small numbers breed in Ireland and so in the summer months our estuaries are almost completely deserted. The birds' wintering and breeding grounds here are coming under increasing pressure from habitat destruction and climate change. The Curlew, an iconic wader known to most people in Ireland, is currently on the brink of extinction as a breeding bird in Ireland.

Ad. Br.

Ad.

Ad. NBr.

m.

chick

uv.

Oystercatcher | Roilleach | *Haematopus ostralegus*
L 40–50cm   WS 80–86cm   AY   CB   Estuary/Coast/Farmland

A bit bigger than Rook; sexes similar. **Adult**: black and white with long, straight, orange-red beak; fairly long, pink legs; white half collar in NBr plumage. **Juv/Im**: a dark tip to the beak, white half collar on 1st S. **In flight**: long, straight, orange-red beak, black-and-white body and wings. **Voice**: a very loud, single-noted piping call, repeated often and sometimes speeding up at the end. Sometimes several birds form a loose circle, calling with necks stretched outward and upward, and beaks pointing towards the ground.

Br. M.

NBr.

1st W.

chick

Lapwing | Pilibín | *Vanellus vanellus*
L 28–31cm   WS 70–76cm   A/W/Sp   SB   Estuary/Wetland/Farmland

Smaller than Oystercatcher; upright posture; sexes similar. **All ages:** thin crest on top
of head, longer on male; glossy iridescent black back/wings; small white patches
on outer four primaries; orange-brown vent/undertail coverts; white belly; black
breast; complex black-and-white face pattern; white tail with black centre; short,
straight, black beak; long, pink-red legs; recently fledged birds have very short crest,
pale edging to back feathers. **In flight:** broad, rounded, dark wings with white tips;
floppy wingbeat; sometimes in large flocks. **Voice:** call is unmistakeable, eerie,
squeaky *peewit*, like a squeaky rubber duck; song similar but more elaborate.

d. feigning
jury

Br.

NBr.

Juv.

Ad. Br.

old chick

young chick

Ringed Plover | Feadóg an fháinne | *Charadrius hiaticula*
L 18–20cm **WS** 48–57cm AY CB Coast/Estuary

Smaller than Redshank; sexes similar. **Adult Br**: distinctive head/breast pattern; forehead white, surrounded by black face mask; white supercilium and neck collar; black breast band; sandy-brown upperparts, white underside; beak short/stubby, orange with black tip; legs pale orange-red. **Adult NBr**: black Br plumage becomes greyish brown; indistinct breast band; dark beak. **Juv/Im**: thin, pale edging to back/wing feathers; all-dark beak; yellowish-brown legs; incomplete breast band. **In flight**: white edge to short dark tail; white wing bar. **Voice**: call is loud, clear, soft *perr-ip*. Song includes rapid, muted *ti-wou*, repeated many times for several seconds/lowering in pitch towards end.

Br. F.

Br. M.

Br. F.

NBr.

Grey Plover

Golden Plover | Feadóg bhuí | *Pluvialis apricaria*
L 27–29cm WS 65–72cm A/W/Sp RB Estuary/Farmland/Upland

Smaller than Oystercatcher; sexes similar; stands very erect; often in very large flocks on fields/estuaries. **Br**: black below with white border; less black on female; yellow, golden-brown; black flecking on back/wings; dark primaries/secondaries. **NBr**: pale grey-brown below, no striking features. **Juv/Im**: similar to NBr adults. **In flight**: faint white wing stripe but looks plain from above at distance, brown head/breast, pale belly/undertail/underwing; rapid wingbeats, rarely alone, usually in large flocks. **Voice**: call is weak-sounding, piping *purr-wee*; song is more elaborate/generally higher pitched. (See Grey Plover p. 125.)

Br. M.

NBr.

NBr.

NBr.

Juv.

NBr.

Golden Plover

Grey Plover | Feadóg ghlas | *Pluvialis squatarola*
L 28cm   WS 76–80cm   A/W/Sp   NB   Estuary

Size of Redshank, sexes similar; lacks yellow plumage colours of Golden Plover,
p. 124; looks monochrome; upright posture, dumpy looking; large, dark eye; short,
thick, straight, dark beak; long, dark grey legs. **Br**: black underparts, white side of
neck/breast/vent/undertail coverts; chequered black-and-white plumage on back/
wings. **NBr**: pale grey below. **In flight**: black 'armpits' (axillaries); white wing stripe;
white on tail; flight direct, rapid. **Voice**: call heard on the ground/in flight is a fairly
high-pitched, drawn-out, plaintive *que-eeeee*, starting on one note, dipping to
a lower one in middle, then up to a higher note at end. (See Golden Plover
p. 124.)

Knot | Cnota | *Calidris canutus*
L 23–25cm WS 58–60cm A/W/Sp NB Estuary/Coast

Slightly smaller/plumper-looking than Redshank; sexes similar; short, olive-green legs; short, slightly curved, dark beak. **NBr**: grey upperparts; pale underside with dark streaking on breast; rump barred; tail grey. Wings/back look scaly at close range, especially juveniles. **Br**: red-orange underparts, flecks of rusty red on back/wings. **In flight NBr**: no obvious markings, grey with fine, indistinct, white wing stripe broadening out towards the wing tips/dark primary coverts; flies with rapid wingbeats; sometimes seen in large flocks. **Voice**: call is high-pitched *whick-whick-whick* often repeated over and over; also a lower-pitched *knuuutt* sound. (See Golden Plover p. 124.)

Br.

NBr.

1st W.

Br.

Br.

Juv.

Juv.

Juv. moulting to 1st W.

Dunlin | Breacóg | *Calidris alpina*
L 16–22cm WS 35–40cm A/W/Sp SB Estuary/Coast

About the size of a Starling; sexes similar; relatively long, thin, slightly downcurved, dark beak, relatively long, dark legs. **Br**: black belly patch and bright brown back. **NBr**: no distinctive features, lacks the black belly patch, overall grey above/white below. **Juv/Im**: two thin white Vs on the back, dark streaks and spots on the breast and sides of the belly. **In flight**: no striking features, dark line down centre of upper tail, thin white wing stripes, black belly patch in Br. plumage. Flies with rapid wingbeats; direct flight. (See Purple Sandpiper p. 139, Curlew Sandpiper p. 144.)

Sanderling | Luathrán/Laidhrín geal | *Calidris alba*
L 20–21cm   WS 41–43cm   A/W/Sp   NB   Coast/Estuary here

About size of a Starling; sexes similar; short, fairly thick, straight, black beak/legs. One of the few waders that can be identified by its feeding behaviour (often runs up/down a sandy beach following the waves in/out). **NBr**: small, white-looking wader, sometimes showing black 'shoulders', pale grey upperparts, white underside. **Br**: orange-red head/breast, rarely seen in full breeding plumage in Ireland. **Juv/Im**: black streaks on back; dark speckling on wings. **In flight**: pale body; dark wings with broad, white wing bar. **Voice**: usually silent on ground but sometimes gives repeated, fairly high-pitched *weeek* call in flight.

Common Sandpiper | Gobadán | *Actitis hypoleucos*
L 18–20cm   WS 35–40cm   Sp/Su/A   CB   Estuary/Wetland

Starling-sized; sexes similar; often bobs its tail; long, straight, dark-tipped grey beak; dark eye; white eye ring; long yellow-green legs; grey-brown smudge on side of breast; white belly/undertail; grey-brown upperparts; white outer-tail feathers barred black. **Br**: fine, dark-brown flecks on head/breast/back/rump. **NBr**: duller plumage. **Juv/Im**: similar to adult but pale tips/edges to feathers (scaly appearance). **In flight**: distinctive; dark upper wings with white stripe; often flying low over water; bursts of fluttering, stiff wingbeats interspersed with short glides, wings rarely lifted above body. **Voice**: loud, high-pitched *Tu-wee hee hee*/long high-pitched whistles usually heard in flight when disturbed.

in courtship flight

Snipe | Mionnán aeir | *Gallinago gallinago*
L 25–27cm   WS 38–48cm   AY   CB   Wetland/Estuary

Bit bigger than Starling; sexes similar; long, straight, dark, downward-pointing beak; stout, dark legs; big feet. **All ages**: black/buff head stripes; body a complex combination of light/dark-brown, black, buff, white; barred flanks; pale belly. **In flight**: will take off at speed in zig-zag flight pattern, then straight line once high off ground; looks dull in bad light. **Voice**: makes short, harsh, rasping call, often repeated. Song is loud, repetitive *tchic-ca*, like rotating squeaky wheel. During display flight, will fly from a height towards ground with its tail fully spread, making rapid, repetitive, bleating sound. (See Jack Snipe p. 142, Long-billed Dowitcher p. 144.)

Woodcock | Creabhar | *Scolopax rusticola*
L 34–36cm WS 56–60cm A/W/Sp SB Woodland

About the size of a Jackdaw, p. 228; much larger than Snipe, p. 130; sexes similar. **All ages**: stout bodied, long straight beak, broad black bars on the crown and brown barring on pale underside of the body. **In flight**: heavy looking, no obvious markings, rusty-brown rump, complex patterns of shades of brown on the body and broad wings, long, straight, downward-pointing beak. **Voice**: usually silent.

Black-tailed Godwit | Guilbneach earrdhubh | *Limosa limosa*
L 41–43cm   WS 75–77cm   A/W/Sp   RB   Estuary/Wetland

Smaller than a Curlew. **Br:** chestnut-red underside; black bars on the flanks and belly, white on vent and undertail coverts; mainly black tail. Long, straight, black-tipped, straw-yellow beak. Female: overall paler. **NBr:** mainly uniform pale grey-brown upperparts; pink beak with black tip; pale supercilium between beak and eye. **Juv/Im:** tan wash on the head and breast; dark-spotted brown back. **In flight:** broad white wing stripe; square white rump patch; mainly black tail; straight beak. Feet project beyond the tail. Flight straight with rapid wingbeats. (See Bar-tailed Godwit p. 133)

Bar-tailed Godwit | Guilbneach stríocearrach | *Limosa lapponica*
L 38–39cm WS 74–76cm A/W/Sp NB Coast/Estuary

Smaller than Oystercatcher; long, slightly upturned beak; long legs. **Br**: red-brown underside including undertail; tail is white with dark bars. Female: pale orange on throat and breast, white belly, vent and undertail coverts. **NBr**: streaked-looking grey back; pale underside. **In flight**: plain wings, darker towards the tips; white triangular rump patch; barred tail. (See Black-tailed Godwit p. 132, Curlew p. 134, Whimbrel p. 135.)

Br. (worn)

NBr.

Juv.

Curlew | Crotach | *Numenius arquata*
L 50–60cm   WS 80–100cm   A/W/Sp   RB Estuary/Wetland/Farmland

Smaller than Great Black-backed Gull; sexes similar; very long, downcurved beak, longer on females; long, blue-grey legs. Usually lacks crown stripes (cf. Whimbrel). **Adult:** brown body and wings with dark streaks and spots; no obvious body or wing markings. **Juv/Im:** finer streaking on the sides of breast and shorter straighter beak. **In flight:** long, curved beak, unmarked wings, triangular pale rump patch, barred tail. **Voice:** can be very noisy, especially when disturbed. A loud *curr-leee* and a bubbly trill are its most characteristic calls. (See Whimbrel p. 135, Bar-tailed Godwit p. 133.)

shorter than
Curlew's

Whimbrel | Crotach eanaigh | *Numenius phaeopus*
L 38–42cm WS 80–84cm Sp/A NB Estuary/Coast/Wetland

Smaller than Curlew; sexes similar; looks like a Curlew but with a shorter, curved beak and a noticeable pale median crown stripe and dark lateral crown stripes . **In flight**: relatively short beak, colour and pattern from above similar to Curlew but looks darker on the outer wing,, triangular white rump patch, barred tail. **Voice**: distinctive call; a fairly high-pitched, flute-like note repeated several times in quick succession. (See Curlew p. 134, Bar-tailed Godwit p. 133.)

Greenshank | Laidhrín glas | *Tringa nebularia*
L 32cm WS 69cm A/W/Sp RB Estuary

A bit bigger than Redshank; sexes similar; fairly long, slightly upturned, dark-tipped grey beak; long, olive-green legs. **NBr**: head/neck looks pale; grey back/wings with no obvious markings; streaks and spots on neck and breast; belly/undertail white. **Br**: becomes more streaked and spotted below and some dark feathers on the back and wings. **Juv/Im**: darker on the back and wings. **In flight**: dark wings and triangular white patch on rump and back; tail white with some faint, fine barring. **Voice**: can be very noisy if disturbed. Usually makes a loud *tchew-tchew-tchew* sound, usually in flight and often repeated.

Redshank | Cosdeargán | *Tringa totanus*
L 27–29cm WS 45–52cm A/W/Sp SB Estuary/Wetland

Smaller than Oystercatcher; sexes similar; long, orange-red legs; medium-sized, straight, dark beak with red base. **NBr:** plain, dark grey-brown upperparts; pale grey-brown on neck/breast; white on belly/undertail. **Br:** heavily streaked on neck/breast/flanks and dark spots on wings/back. **Juv/Im:** more vividly marked than NBr adults; yellow-orange legs. **In flight:** triangular white patch on back and broad white trailing edge to most of wing. White tail with dark bars, feet project a little beyond the tail. **Voice:** very noisy when disturbed; utters a loud, harsh, repeated *tieuu-ieuu*. In the breeding season it makes a monotonous, repeating *tiew-tiew-tiew* sound. (See Spotted Redshank p. 146.)

Turnstone | Piardálaí trá | *Arenaria interpres*
L 22–23cm   WS 46cm   A/W/Sp   NB   Coast/Estuary

Size of Starling; sexes similar; low profile when on ground; short, orange legs; dark, stubby, pointed beak; often reluctant to fly, preferring to walk or run away; rarely seen alone. **NBr:** dark grey-brown upperparts/breast patches, white belly. **Br:** distinctive black-and-white head/breast; complex orange/brown/black back pattern. **Juv/Im:** similar to NBr but pale edges to wing/back. **In flight:** upperparts form a striking pattern of browns/black/white. Flies fast/straight, usually low over water. **Voice:** calls in flight/on ground; variable but include rapidly repeated *tuck-tuck-tuck* often rising in pitch/speed towards end. Lower piping notes also heard. (See Purple Sandpiper p. 139.)

1st W.

1st W.

Br.

NBr.

1st W.

1st W.

1st W.

1st W.

Purple Sandpiper | Gobadán cosbhuí | *Calidris maritima*
L 20–22cm WS 43–45cm A/W/Sp NB Coast

Smaller than Redshank; sexes similar; relatively long, stout, orange-yellow legs;
short, slightly downcurved, orange-yellow beak with dark tip; likes open rocky
shore; purple sheen to plumage. **Adult**: dark grey-brown upperparts/head; pale
underside with heavy streaking on breast/flanks. **Juv/Im**: pale edges to wing feathers;
looks brighter than adults. **In flight**: fast and direct; overall dark grey from above,
darkest on rump/tail; very thin white wing stripe; paler below with white on
underwing/towards undertail. **Voice**: not very vocal in winter, often only making
a high-pitched, twittering call when disturbed. (See Turnstone p. 138; Dunlin
p. 127, Curlew Sandpiper p. 144.)

M. moulting
out of breeding plumage

NBr. M.

Juv.

Juv:

Ju

Ruff | Rufachán | *Philomachus pugnax*
L 22–30cm WS 48–58cm Sp/A NB Estuary/Wetland

A bit bigger than Redshank; relatively short, slightly downcurved beak; long, orange-yellow legs. **NBr:** sexes similar; erect posture; pale around base of beak; dark crown; scaly brown upperparts; pale buff neck/breast; white belly/vent/undertail coverts. **Br Male:** long collar (ruff) of feathers of varying colour; round tufts on head; black feathers on throat and breast. Birds in this plumage are rarely seen in Ireland. **Juv/Im:** more vividly marked than adult; scaled appearance to back/wings. **In flight:** dark upperparts with white V-shaped border to rump feathers; feet project beyond tail; thin white wing stripe. **Voice:** usually silent. (See Buff-breasted Sandpiper p. 146.)

Scarce & Rare

Avocet

Glossy Ibis

Avocet | Abhóiséad | *Recurvirostra avosetta*
L 42–46cm   WS 68–76   A/W/Sp   NB   Estuary

Unmistakeable when seen at close range. About the size of an Oystercatcher,
p. 121. Black-and-white plumage, slender upturned beak and long blue-grey legs.
Immature birds have some brown on back and wings. At a distance could be
mistaken for a Shelduck (p. 44) or even a gull. Feeds by sweeping its beak from
side to side on water.

Glossy Ibis | Íbis niamhrach | *Plegadis falcinellus*
L 55–65cm   WS 90–100cm   Sp/A   NB   Wetland/Farmland

A little bit like an all-dark Curlew, p. 134; long, curved beak; dark, glossy plumage,
duller on young birds; unlike Curlew, legs project well beyond the tail when in flight.

Note: Images not to scale

Scarce & Rare *(cont'd)*

Grey Phalarope | Falaróp gobmhór | *Phalaropus fulicarius*
L 20–22   WS 38–44cm   A   NB   Sea/Coast

Dunlin-sized; very similar to Red-necked Phalarope (below). **Adult NBr**: uniform grey upperparts; white underside; thin neck, small head; relatively long, very thin beak, thicker than Red-necked; dark patch behind eye and back of the crown. **Br**: brick-red below; yellow beak; black crown; white face mask. In Ireland usually see **Juv/Im**, which is darker on the back and back of the crown.

Red-necked Phalarope | Falaróp gobchaol | *Phalaropus lobatus*
L 17–19cm   WS 30–36cm   A   RB   Wetland/Estuary

Dunlin-sized; very similar to Grey Phalarope (above). **Adult NBr**: striped and scaly grey upperparts; white underside; thin neck, small head; relatively long very thin beak; dark patch behind eye and some on back of the crown. **Br**: white throat, orange-red side of neck and upper breast. In Ireland we usually see **Juv/Im**, which are darker on the back and crown. The species previously bred in Ireland and some have attempted in recent times.

Jack Snipe | Naoscach bhídeach | *Lymnocryptes minimus*
L 18–20cm   WS 35–40cm   W   NB   Wetland/Estuary

Smaller than Snipe, p. 130; very similar plumage but does not have pale central crown stripe; shorter beak only slightly longer than the horizontal length of the head; pale stripes on the back very noticeable; very reluctant to fly. More direct flight than Snipe and rarely flies very far.

Grey Phalarope

Grey Phalarope

Br. M.

Br. F.

Red-necked Phalarope

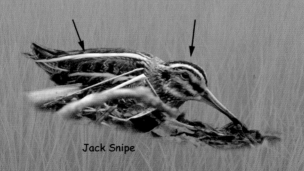

Jack Snipe

Note: Images not to scale

Scarce & Rare *(cont'd)*

Little Stint | Gobadáinín beag | *Calidris minuta*
L 13–15cm   WS 30–36cm   A   NB   Coast/Estuary

Tiny wader; can look like a small Sanderling (p. 128) with thin, straight beak; Juv/Im has white 'braces' on the back. Pale around the beak and on the breast; some faint streaking on side of breast.

Curlew Sandpiper | Gobadán crotaigh | *Calidris ferruginea*
L 18–20cm   WS 42–46cm   A   NB   Coast/Estuary

Same size as Dunlin, p. 127: longer, thinner, curved beak; broad, pale supercilium. **Adult Br**: bright red on head/breast/belly. **Adult NBr**: grey upperparts and white underside with only faint streaking on breast. **Juv/Im**: scaly back and wings; pale buff on neck and breast. **In flight**: white rump.

Pectoral Sandpiper | Gobadán uchtach | *Calidris melanotos*
L 19–23cm   WS 42–49cm   A   NB   Coast/Estuary

A bit bigger than a Dunlin, p. 127. **Adult**: finely dark-streaked buff head, neck and breast; clear division between breast and white belly. Long, olive-green legs. **Juv/Im**: brighter plumage and white 'braces' on the back. **In flight**: only faint pale wing stripe.

Long-billed Dowitcher | Guilbnín gobfhada | *Lymnodromus scolopaceus*
L 24–26cm   WS 46–52cm   A/W   NB   Estuary/Wetland

About the size of a Redshank (p. 137) but looks heavier; a bit like a large Snipe (p.130) with a very long, straight, stout beak; broad, bright buff supercilium; no obvious pale stripes on the back or closed wing. **In flight**: long, thin white rump patch; finely barred tail and thin white trailing edge to secondaries and inner primaries. The tertials on the much rarer Short-billed Dowitcher are two-toned and not plain-centred.

Juv.

Juv.

Little Stint

Juv.

Br.

Curlew Sandpiper

Juv.

Juv.

Pectoral Sandpiper

Juv.

Note: Images not to scale

Long-billed Dowitcher

Scarce & Rare *(cont'd)*

Wood Sandpiper | Gobadán coille | *Tringa glareola*
L 19–21cm   WS 45–55cm   A   NB   Wetland/Estuary

Similar in size and plumage to Green Sandpiper (see below); noticeable pale supercilium; brighter greenish-yellow legs; lighter and more diffuse streaking on the breast; narrow dark bars on the tail. Some calls high pitched and a bit like a day-old chick in tone. **In flight:** similar to Green Sandpiper but pale underwing.

Green Sandpiper | Gobadán glas | *Tringa ochropus*
L 20–24cm   WS 40–50cm   A/Sp   NB   Wetland/Estuary

Smaller than Redshank, p. 137; sexes similar; fairly long, thin, straight, dark beak; legs olive green. **All ages:** square white rump patch sometimes visible; short white tail with broad dark bars; dark upperparts with small light spots, pale underside with streaking on the head and breast. **In flight:** looks dark from above with bright white square rump patch; from below, looks pale bodied with all dark wings. (See Wood Sandpiper, above)

Buff-breasted Sandpiper | Gobadán broinn-donnbhuí | *Tryngites subruficollis*
L 18–20cm   WS 43–47cm   A   NB   Coast/Estuary

Like a small female Ruff, p. 140. **All ages:** buff face with indistinct, large, pale eye ring; buff throat, breast and belly; some dark spots on side of breast; long, dull yellow legs. **In flight:** all-dark rump and tail, no obvious wing markings above, white underwing with dark-tipped primary coverts forming a dark line near the wing tip.

Spotted Redshank | Cosdeargán breac | *Tringa erythropus*
L 29–32   WS 61–67cm   Sp/Au   NB   Estuary/Wetlands

Similar to/bigger than Redshank, p. 137; long, thin, straight, dark beak with some red at base; long red-orange legs; sexes similar. **NBr:** grey upperparts with some white spotting on wings; bright white supercilium; black stripe between eye/base of beak; white underside, some grey on side of breast; tail white with fine dark bars. **In flight:** no white trailing edge to wings; long, white, oval patch on rump/back. **Br:** all-dark plumage with fine spotting on back/wings; rarely seen in this plumage in Ireland but some occur when in transition to NBr plumage. **Juv/Im:** darker than NBr; barred below. **Voice:** call short distinctive high *chewee*.

Wood Sandpiper

NBr.

Juv.

Green Sandpiper

Ad.

Green Sandpiper

Juv.

Buff-breasted Sandpiper

Br.

NBr.

Spotted Redshank

Note: Images not to scale

Birds of Prey (Hawks, Falcons, Harriers, Eagles, Buzzard, Owls)

Hawks and falcons are the most common members of this group in Ireland. Hawks tend to have rounded wings and long tails, use surprise attack to catch their prey and feed mainly on birds and also small mammals. Hawks will hunt in woodland and gardens. The Sparrowhawk is the best known of the hawks in this country. Falcons tend to have more pointed wings than hawks and like to hunt in the open. Many falcons catch their prey on the wing but our most familiar falcon, the Kestrel, prefers to hunt small mammals.

Harriers have relatively long wings and tails. They hunt by moving along a field, reed bed, or moor looking for prey on the ground. They 'flap and glide'; a few wingbeats and then glide with the wings held in a shallow 'V'. They feed on small birds and small mammals. The Hen Harrier is the only breeding member of this group in Ireland. The Marsh Harrier bred up to the end of the 19th century and the rare Montague's Harrier has been recorded breeding here on a couple of occasions in the past. The Hen Harrier is declining as a breeding species, probably as a result of loss of good moorland habitat where they breed, and climate change.

Eagles, buzzards and kites will readily eat carrion (dead animals) and also small mammals and even fish, in the case of the White-tailed Sea Eagle. All three were extinct in Ireland as breeding species by the end of the 19th and early 20th centuries, largely due to human persecution. The Buzzard recolonised naturally with a

Kestrel

pair in Antrim in 1933 and has been spreading south and west since then. Eagles and kites, on the other hand, have been the subject of reintroduction programmes in recent decades. The Golden Eagle is being reintroduced in Donegal, the White-tailed Eagle in Kerry and the Red Kite in Wicklow, Dublin and Down. Golden Eagles and Red Kites are once again breeding in the wild in Ireland and White-tailed Eagles are set to breed in the not-too-distant future. The fondness for carrion of all these birds of prey has unfortunately led to some being killed by the illegal use of poison in pieces of meat laid out to kill foxes, etc.

Six species of the owl family have occurred in Ireland, but only two – the Barn Owl and the Long-eared Owl – regularly breed here. They usually hunt at night but will also hunt in daylight hours, especially at dawn and dusk during the breeding season or when food is scarce. They eat mainly small mammals but also small birds. In recent years there has been a dramatic decline in breeding Barn Owls. The cause of decline is not clearly understood and is thought to be a combination of factors, such as habitat loss, secondary poisoning, climate change, etc. The Short-eared Owl is a winter visitor that usually hunts by day and the other three species, including the Snowy Owl, are very rare.

Kestrel | Pocaire gaoithe | *Falco tinnunculus*
L 32–36cm WS 74–78cm AY CB Farmland

Size of Jackdaw. **Male**: grey head; rusty-coloured back; long, grey tail with white-tipped terminal black band. **Female**: red-brown with dark barring on back/wings; dark primaries; pale and streaked underside; tail: brown with dark bars; pale-tipped, dark terminal tail band. **Juv/Im**: similar to female but brighter tones; heavier streaking below. **In flight**: hovers in the one spot, sometimes not flapping its wings if the wind is strong enough. Pointed wings – narrower/more pointed wings than Sparrowhawk – and pale-tipped, black terminal tail band. **Voice**: vocal during breeding season, near its nest. A loud sharp rapid *kee-kee-kee-keee*. (See young Sparrowhawk p. 151, Merlin p. 153.)

Sparrowhawk | Spióróg | *Accipiter nisus*
L 30–34cm WS 60–80cm AY CB Woodland/Farmland/Garden

Jackdaw-sized. **Male:** blue-grey upperparts; orange-brown cheek/upper breast; lower breast/belly barred white and orange-brown; tail broadly barred light/dark grey-brown. **Female:** larger than male; dark grey upperparts; pale supercilium; barred white/dark brown below. **Juv/Im:** dark brown upperparts; pale edges to back/wing coverts, heavily barred dark brown underside. **In flight:** broad, blunt-ended wings; long, slightly rounded tail; rapid wingbeats with short glides; does not hover. **Voice:** varied repertoire during Br. season including loud high *wa-kaa-kaa-kaa*, often repeated. Begging young make a high, squeaking *weee-weee-weee*. Silent outside Br. season. (See Merlin p. 153, Kestrel p. 150, Goshawk p. 160.)

Birds of Prey (Hawks, Falcons, Harriers, Eagles, Buzzard, Owls) | 151

Peregrine | Seabhac seilge | *Falco peregrinus*
L 38–50cm WS 90–100cm AY SB All habitats (from sea cliffs to quarries to towns to upl

Male slightly smaller than Rook and female slightly bigger; sexes similar. **Adult:** slate-grey upperparts; finely barred underside, pale upper breast and throat, dark 'teardrop' below eye. **Juv/Im:** dark brown upperparts, heavily streaked dark brown underside, dark 'teardrop' below eye. **In flight:** look for head pattern, pointed wings, stiff-winged flight. 'Stoops' by closing the wings and descending at great speed to catch prey. **Voice:** includes a high, irritating, squeaking *kaw-kik-kaw-tieu*. Alarm call is a high, drawn-out *kwaugh* cry repeated with variable pitch.

1st W. M.

1st W. M.

1st W. M.

W. M.

Ad. F.

1st W. M.

Ad. M.

F.

Im.

Im.

Merlin | Meirliún | *Falco columbarius*
L26–30cm WS 56–62cm A/W/Sp SB Upland/Farmland

A bit bigger than a Blackbird and smaller than a Kestrel. **Male**: slate-blue on the back and wings, darker towards the wing tips; grey tail with white-tipped, dark terminal band, heavily streaked red-brown on the underside. **Female**: dark brown upperparts; heavily streaked dark brown underside; broad, dark brown bars on the tail. **Juv/Im**: similar to female but more heavily barred wings and tail. **In flight**: agile flier when hunting; pointed wings; smaller and darker than Kestrel. (See Kestrel p. 150, Sparrowhawk p. 151.)

Buzzard | Clamhán | *Buteo buteo*
L 50–56cm WS 120–125cm AY SB (increasing) Farmland/Woodland

Much larger than Sparrowhawk; sexes similar; yellow legs; yellow base to dark hook-tipped beak. **All ages**: broad, fairly blunt-ended wings, 'fingered' primaries; relatively short, broad tail; plumage can vary a lot; adult usually darker than Juv/Im. **In flight**: from below, all show dark wing coverts with indistinct pale underwing covert bar; pale, barred, dark-tipped primaries and secondaries; finely barred tail with black terminal bar on adults; soars with few wing flaps. **Voice**: call is a drawn-out, high-pitched *Keeere* sound, often heard in flight, especially in spring and early summer.

Juv.

Ad.

Juv.

Ad.

Juv.

Juv.

Juv.

Red Kite | Cúr rua | *Milvus milvus*
L 60–70cm WS 145–160cm AY RB Farmland

A bit bigger than Herring Gull; long, forked tail and long, narrow wings. **Adult:** bright red-brown tail above, paler below. Red-brown body with dark streaks, pale head. **Im:** Not as brightly coloured, paler body, particularly on the undertail. **In flight:** from above, bright red on tail, which looks forked when closed and almost straight ended when spread; from below, large pale patch on the primaries with dark wing tips. **Voice:** usually silent. Makes a high-pitched, thin call of about six notes, the first drawn out. Being reintroduced in Wicklow, Dublin and Down, and is spreading.

Juv.

2nd W. M.

Ad. M.

Ad. M.

Juv.

Ad.

Juv.

Ad. F.

Ad. F.

Hen Harrier | Cromán na gcearc | *Circus cyaneus*
L 46–50cm WS 108–112cm AY SB but becoming RB Upland/Woodland/Wetland

A bit bigger than Rook; long, yellow legs, stubby hook-tipped beak. **Male**: uniform grey body/wings with black outer primaries; white rump patch; long, grey tail. **Female**: brown, streaked below, white rump patch; long, barred tail. **Juv/Im**: similar to adult female; irises usually dark; from below in flight has dark inner secondaries. Young male in 2nd Y resembles adult but has brown feathers on the wings. **In flight**: long, narrow wings and tail, square white rump patch; glides a lot with wings' help in a shallow 'V'. (See Marsh Harrier p. 160.)

Barn Owl | Scréachóg reilige | *Tyto alba*
L 33–36cm WS 87–90cm AY SB Farmland

About the size of a Jackdaw; sexes similar. **All ages**: flat, white, heart-shaped face; large, black eyes; deep yellow-buff upperparts with small dark and light flecks; underside white; legs long with large, taloned feet; looks 'knock-kneed' when perched; no ear tufts. **In flight**: silent; looks pale; blunt head; short tail; wings broad and round-tipped; wingbeats jerky and stiff. Glides and hovers; legs sometimes hang down when hunting. **Voice**: the quietest of our owls but occasionally makes a loud shriek, does not hoot. The young make a hissing noise.

Long-eared Owl | Ceann cait | *Asio otus*
L 35–37cm WS 93–97cm AY CB Woodland/Farmland/Urban parks

Jackdaw-sized; sexes similar. **All ages**: long 'ear' tufts, orange iris; complex light/
dark brown-patterned upperparts; grey/white spots on inner wing; underside
light brown/heavy dark streaking; slim upright posture. **In flight**: pale underwing
with black mark at 'elbow'; dark barred outer primaries. From above, mottled dark
brown, primaries buff with dark bars at tips/primary coverts forming dark patch.
Long, blunt-tipped wings, short tail, blunt head. Usually flies at night/dusk/dawn; very
stiff, jerky flight. **Voice**: during breeding season male makes a low moaning *whoo-
oooo-oooo* call, also squeaks/clapping sounds. Fledged Juv makes a sound like a
creaking gate. (See Short-eared Owl p. 159.)

Short-eared Owl | Ulchabhán réisc | *Asio flammeus*
L 36–40cm WS 98–104cm A/W/Sp NB Coast/Estuary

Slightly smaller than Rook; sexes similar. **All ages**: yellow iris, tiny 'ear' tufts, body coarsely mottled light and dark brown. **In flight**: from below, pale wings with black wing tips and mark at the 'elbow', streaking on neck and breast only. **Juv**: birds just out of the nest are light and dark grey; downy with yellow irises. **In flight**: white trailing edge to the wing; black wing tips; faintly streaked pale belly. Stiff wingbeats and glides. Often seen hunting in broad daylight and regularly seen on the ground. (See Long-eared Owl p. 158.)

Scarce & Rare

Snowy Owl | Ulchabhán sneachtúil | *Bubo scandiacus*
L 54–64cm   WS 130–160cm   A/W/Sp   NB/RB   Upland/Coast

Much larger than Barn Owl, p. 157; adult male all white; adult female white with dark tips to body and wing feathers. Flies during the day and likes open ground without trees or shrubs.

Marsh Harrier | Cromán móna | *Circus aeruginosus*
L 43–55cm   WS 115–135cm   Sp/A   NB/RB   Wetland

Same size as Hen Harrier (p. 156) but longer wings; no white rump. **Adult male**: brown on some wing coverts and back; dark streaking on breast and belly. **Adult female**: overall dark with pale brown head with thick, dark eye stripe, pale shoulder patches. **Juv/Im**: looks all dark with bright cream-brown head and thick, dark eye stripe.

Goshawk | Spioróg mhór | *Accipiter gentilis*
L 48–60cm   WS 110–140cm   A/W/Sp   RB   Woodland

Like a large Sparrowhawk, p. 151. **Adult**: prominent, long, white supercilium; dark crown and cheek; shorter broader tail. **Juv/Im**: more obvious pale flecking on the upperparts and distinct dark stripes on breast and belly.

im. M.

F.

Snowy Owl

Marsh Harrier

Ad. F.

Ad. M.

Goshawk (Juv.)

Note: Images not to scale

Osprey | Coirneach | *Pandion haliaetus*
L 54–60cm   WS 150–170cm   Sp/A   NB   Wetland/Estuary

Small eagle; looks black and white from below. White head with thick, dark eye stripe; dark brown upperparts, scaly looking on Juv/Im. White underside with indistinct breast markings; white underwing coverts with dark trailing edge to secondary coverts on adults; hovers over water and plunge dives for fish.

White-tailed Eagle | Iolar mara | *Haliaeetus albicilla*
L 70–90cm   WS 195–245cm   AY   NB/RB   Coast/Estuary/Wetland

Huge bird of prey; similar in shape and size to Golden Eagle; long, broad wings with long primary 'fingers'. Massive hooked beak; plumage variable and changes over three years, beginning dark brown with dark-bordered pale tail feathers; becomes paler on adults, especially on the head and breast with white tail; bill starts dark grey and becomes yellow. Release programme in Kerry.

Golden Eagle | Iolar | *Aquila chrysaetos*
L 78–90cm   WS 195–225cm   AY   RB   Upland/Coast

Huge bird of prey; similar in shape and size to White-tailed Eagle. **Adult**: overall dark brown; broadly and indistinctly barred dark tail. **Juv/Im**: white patches on outer wing; white tail with broad black terminal band; plumage darkens with age; reaches adult plumage after four or five years. Reintroduction programme in Donegal.

Osprey

White-tailed Eagle (Im.)

White-tailed Eagle (Ad.)

Golden Eagle (Ad.)

Note: Images not to scale

Pheasant

Pheasant, Red Grouse, Grey Partridge, Quail

All members of this group in Ireland are referred to as 'game birds'. This is because they are either hunted with guns today or were hunted in the past. They all have short, stubby beaks, relatively large, round bodies and strong, short legs. They are all ground-loving birds and usually only fly if they feel they are in danger, although prefer to run away under cover. All habitually nest on the ground and their diet consists of seeds and other vegetable matter as well as insects.

The only common member of this group in Ireland is the Pheasant, which was introduced into Ireland probably in the 16th century from the Caucasus and later from China. The Red Grouse in Ireland is considered a separate race of Red Grouse from others in its range, along with birds of western and northern Britain and Scotland. It is also considered to be declining in numbers.

The Grey Partridge is now found only in County Offaly. It was once widespread in Ireland but changes in farming practices in the last 60 years have led to its dramatic decline. It is the subject of a long-term project to increase its population and distribution.

The Quail is the only migratory member of the group, spending the winter in Africa. Like the Grey Partridge, it too has suffered a dramatic decline in population, again through changes in farming practices since the 1950s, along with increased hunting pressure along its migration routes across the Mediterranean.

missing tail

Pheasant | Coilleach coille | *Phasianus colchicus*
L 60–90cm WS 78–82cm AY CB Farmland

About the size of a Rook, excluding the tail; pale, hook-tipped beak. **Male**: very long, pointed tail; red face; dark head, sometimes has white neck ring. **Female**: long, pointed tail, all plumage mottled light and dark browns. **Juv/Im**: like female with shorter tail. **In flight**: long, pointed tail, rounded wings, rapid wingbeats make a whirring sound, rarely flies far. Usually seen on the ground, flying only when disturbed or going to roost; may not fly until you are very close. **Voice**: cock makes a loud, short, hoarse *chalk-chalk* or *chaw-huck*. (See Corncrake p.119)

Red Grouse | Cearc fhraoigh | *Lagopus lagopus*
L 36–40cm WS 60cm AY SB Upland

Slightly smaller than Rook; pheasant/chicken-like bird of open upland areas. **Male:** bright red crests over the eyes; white eye ring; mottled, rich-brown plumage with a short, dark, round-ended tail; short legs covered in pale feathers. **Female:** lacks red crests and has paler plumage. **In flight:** looks dull from above with no obvious markings. Usually only flies when disturbed. Rises fairly quickly, staying fairly low; also glides on bowed wings. **Voice:** makes strange duck-like sounds including a phrase with the tempo of a spinning coin coming to a stop. (See female Pheasant p. 165.)

Scarce & Rare

F.

M.

Grey Partridge | Patraisc | *Perdix perdix*
L 28–31cm WS 45–48cm   AY   RB (also being released)   Farmland

Fat-looking; a bit smaller than a Jackdaw. **Male**: grey head, breast; orange-brown face; dark brown belly patch; brown bars on grey flanks. **Female**: duller with smaller or no belly patch; **Juv/Im**: all brown with dark and light streaking on flanks. **In flight**: from above, no obvious marking, short reddish-brown tail; rapid wingbeats and glides, reluctant to fly.

Quail | Gearg | *Coturnix coturnix*
L 16–18cm WS 32–35cm   Sp/Su/A   RB   Farmland

Slightly smaller than a Starling. **All ages**: brown and buff with light and dark streaking on the flanks and back; male has black throat and cream-and-black markings on the head. **In flight**: very short tail; rapid wingbeats; no obvious markings; very reluctant to fly. **Voice**: male makes a high-pitched fast fluid *whit whit-whit* sound (See Corncrake p. 119)

> Note: Images not to scale

Doves, Pigeons, Cuckoo and Nightjar

Collared Dove

Doves and pigeons are characterised by very short legs, small heads and cooing calls. The most common member of this group is the Woodpigeon, which can be a serious pest to farmers. The most recent arrival is the Collared Dove, unheard of here before 1959, and now widespread and common.

Four cuckoo species have been recorded in Ireland. The most common is the Cuckoo, which comes here every summer and lays its eggs in another bird's nest, leaving the foster parents to raise their outsized lodger. One south European and two American species of cuckoo have also been reported in Ireland.

Only one member of the nightjar family is found in Ireland. This is the Nightjar, an insect-eating summer visitor from Africa. It is very scarce, nesting usually in open woodland. Like other members of this group, it is nocturnal. It has long wings and tail, and its plumage provides perfect camouflage during the day when it is resting on the ground or in a tree.

Juv.

Ad.

Woodpigeon | Colm coille | *Columba palumbus*
L 40–42cm WS 75–80cm AY CB Woodland/Farmland/Garden

Rook-sized; fat-looking; small head; short, red legs; pale yellow/pink beak; pale cream iris; overall grey body. **Adult**: white neck patches/crescents on wings; pink-grey breast; rump/lower back pale blue-grey; tail is grey with black band, more clearly marked below. **Juv/Im**: as adult, but lacks white on neck. **In flight**: grey, white crescents on wing; rapid wingbeats; can be mistaken for bird of prey. Display: steep flight upwards, ending in loud wing claps and downward glide. **Voice**: loud cooing, sounding like *Take two, John, take two*; often repeated several times/may start in middle of phrase. (See Stock Dove p. 170, Rock Dove/Feral Pigeon p. 171.)

Stock Dove | Colm gorm | *Columba oenas*
L 30–33cm WS 63–66cm AY CB Farmland

Size of Jackdaw; sexes similar. **Adult**: no white plumage. Blue-grey head/back, pink on neck/breast with iridescent green patch on side of neck; light grey rump/tail; broad, black terminal tail band; red beak/yellow tip; dark pink legs. **Juv/Im**: paler than adult; dark beak; no green on neck; brown wash on wings. **In flight**: dark grey with black secondaries/primaries; paler grey wing panel; dark grey inner wing; black tips to innermost secondary coverts; faster wingbeats than Woodpigeon. **Voice**: soft cooing *awoooa*, may be repeated many times. Beware: Feral Pigeons can look similar. (See Woodpigeon p. 169, Rock Dove/Feral Pigeon p. 171.)

Rock Dove

Rock Dove

Rock Dove

ock Dove

Rock Dove

Rock Dove

al Pigeon

Feral Pigeon

Feral Pigeon

Feral Pigeon

Feral Pigeon

Rock Dove/Feral Pigeon | Colm aille | *Columba livia*
L 30–34cm WS 62–64cm AY RB/CB Coast (Feral Pigeons – Urban/Suburban/Coast)

About size of Jackdaw; pure wild Rock Doves are now rare due to interbreeding with Feral Pigeon, which are their descendants. Stubby dark beak/dark pink legs. **Rock Dove (all ages)**: white rump; grey back/wings, two black wing bars; darker grey head/breast with iridescent green/pink. **In flight**: white rump; grey wing with broad black trailing edge; thin, black wing bar; silvery underwing, black trailing edge; dark head; grey tail with narrow black terminal band. **Feral Pigeons**: mainly racing pigeons that revert to breeding wild; all colours/patterns. **Voice**: cooing sounds. (See Stock Dove p. 170, Woodpigeon p. 169.)

Juv.

Ad.

Collared Dove | Fearán baicdhubh | *Streptopelia decaocto*
L 30–32cm WS 49–53cm AY CB Farmland/Garden

Slightly smaller than Jackdaw; sexes similar; short, thin, dark beak; dark red eye; short, powdery-pink legs. **All ages**: sandy-brown plumage; dark brown primaries; distinctive (but not always noticeable) thin, black half-collar at base of neck; recently fledged birds have no half collar. **In flight**: sandy-brown; darker wing tips; pale tips to most tail feathers, large, white undertail band. Flies straight with fast, jerky wingbeats. Display: glides with stiff, slightly downcurved wings/fanned tail, showing pale under-wing/white undertail with black band at base. **Voice**: a gentle cooing sound phrased like '*can yoouuu coo*' repeated twice or more. (See Turtle Dove p. 174)

Ad.

Juv.

Cuckoo | Cuach | *Cuculus canorus*
L 32–35cm WS 55–62cm Sp/Su/A SB Wetland/Farmland

About size of Jackdaw; short, slightly downcurved beak; short, yellow legs. **Male:** grey head/breast/back; long, dark grey, white-tipped, round-ended tail; barred belly/undertail; dark plain wings. **Female:** variable amounts of barring/buff on breast. In some rare instances, females can have brown upperparts/pale underside with dark barring all over. **Juv/Im:** white spot on nape; variable amounts of brown on head/back/wings; thin white edges to some feathers on back/wings; hawk-like. Fluttering wingbeats, wings rarely lifted above body. Usually glides briefly before landing. **Voice:** male makes classic *cuck-oo*; female makes a high, rapid, bubbling sound.

Scarce & Rare

Turtle Dove | Colm fearán | *Streptopelia turtur*
L 26–28cm WS 46–52cm A NB Farmland/Garden

Same size and shape as Collared Dove (p. 172) but looks darker overall; dark-centred, pale brown scapular and inner wing covert feathers give scaled appearance on closed wing; black-and-white gill pattern on side of neck; tail is dark grey-brown deepening to black with white tips and edges; pink-grey on head and breast; pale belly. **Voice**: rapid, soft, purring sound, repeated.

Nightjar | Tuirne lín | *Caprimulgus europaeus*
L 25–28cm WS 54–62cm S RB Woodland

Unmistakeable, about the size of a blackbird with long wings; dark 'dead bark' plumage; tiny beak. Rests on branches or the ground during the day and starts hunting at dusk. **In flight**: white patches on the primaries and on the end of the square-ended tail.

> Note: Images not to scale

Kingfisher, Woodpecker, Hoopoe and Bee-eater

Kingfishers are found all around the world, especially in tropical areas. Our kingfisher nests in a burrow at the riverside. The American Belted Kingfisher has also been seen in Ireland but on only a few occasions.

Kingfisher

Woodpeckers are generally very rare visitors to Ireland, despite the fact that four species breed as close as Britain. Only one species, the Great Spotted Woodpecker, has recently started breeding here and is spreading from its first breeding areas on the east of the island. If it continues to expand at its current rate, it could become a familiar sight in our woodlands and gardens. The main reason they are so rare here is that British/European woodpeckers do not usually migrate. It is thought that Ireland became cut off from Britain and the rest of Europe before woodpeckers had a chance to colonise this island. There is also a suggestion that they were here before but became extinct following the removal of our forests. In fact, two of the five species of woodpecker on record are from North America, where some woodpeckers are migratory, while a number of European species, breeding much closer to Ireland, have yet to be seen here.

The Hoopoe is usually a spring visitor to Ireland, occurring in small numbers every year. It breeds in southern Europe and some overshoot when migrating north from their African wintering grounds. It usually feeds on insects, which it catches on the ground.

Bee-eaters are related to the kingfishers. They are very colourful birds associated with southern Europe and Africa as well as Asia and Australia. As the name suggests, they eat insects, including bees, which they catch on the wing. They nest in burrows, usually in sandy cliffs. The European Bee-eater is usually found in southern Europe and only reaches our shores when birds migrating north from their African wintering grounds overshoot their breeding grounds in southern Europe, usually in spring.

Kingfisher | Cruidín | *Alcedo atthis*
L 16–18cm WS 24–26cm AY CB Wetland

Smaller than a Starling; sexes similar. **All ages**: metallic, pale blue back; orange breast and belly; white neck patch; short, rounded sky-blue wings with white spots on the inner half; dagger-shaped beak; very short pink-red legs. The male has an all-dark beak and female has orange-red towards the base of the lower mandible. **In flight**: like a blue flash; low, straight, buzzing flight with occasional gliding; dives from branches and other perches over water; can be seen on the coast in winter. **Voice**: its call is a very loud, piercing *pseeeeee*, often repeated several times, usually in flight.

Ad. M.

Ad. F.

F.

Ad. M.

Ad. M.

Great Spotted Woodpecker | Mórchnagaire breac | *Dendrocopos major*
L 22–25cm   WS 35–42cm   AY   RB (increasing)   Woodland/Garden

About size of Blackbird; creeps up tree trunks/branches; fairly long, pointed dark beak; short grey legs; two toes point forward/two backward; visits garden peanut feeders. **Adult:** black-and-white upperparts, large white patch on wing; white underside; bright red vent/undertail coverts; red patch on nape, absent in female; long, pointed black tail, white spots on sides. **Juv/Im:** male has red cap, less obvious on female; pink vent/undertail coverts. **In flight:** black upperparts; white spots on primaries/secondaries; two oval white patches at base of wings; long, pointed tail, white spots on edges; pronounced undulating flight. **Voice:** a short, squeaky *cheep*, drumming on trees sounds like creaking door.

Hoopoe | Húpú | *Upupa epops*
L 26–28cm WS 43–47cm Sp NB Farmland/Coast/Coastal Gardens

Unmistakeable, about the size of a Blackbird; pinkish orange head and breast with large head crest, which has black tips to the feathers and which is usually kept flat but is sometimes raised; black-and-white striped and barred wings, back and tail; wings broad and rounded, long, thin, downcurved beak.

Bee-eater | Beachadóir Eorpach | *Merops apiaster*
L 26–29cm WS 38–44cm Sp NB Coast

Unmistakeable, about the size of a Blackbird, brightly coloured; relatively long, thin, curved beak; yellow throat and pale blue breast and belly; yellow and orange-brown on head, back and inner wing above; long, plain tail with longer, pointed central tail feathers.

> Note: Images not to scale

Swallows, Martins and Swift

Swift

Swallows and martins are closely related. The term 'swallow' is usually used for long-tailed members of the group while 'martin' is used for short-tailed members. They are summer migrants from Africa to Ireland, arriving here in spring and departing in autumn. If the weather is good they will often rear two or even three broods of young. They all spend most of their time on the wing and feed exclusively on insects, which they catch in flight. The Swallow and House Martin use mud and saliva to make a cup-shaped nest while the Sand Martin digs a burrow in sandy cliffs, often in sand quarries. Swallows usually nest in covered areas such as inside barns, sheds and outhouses while House Martins usually build their nests on the outside of buildings. Natural breeding sites for these birds include caves and cliffs.

While not closely related to swallows and martins, Swifts share their aerial existence and are members of a group of birds that spend almost all their life on the wing and are summer visitors to Ireland from Africa. They come here only to lay their eggs and rear there young in cavities under the eaves of big buildings. They are so adapted to an aerial existence that they cannot take off from level ground or perch on a wire or twig. Their tiny feet and claws are designed for clinging onto vertical surfaces. Like the other members of this group, the Swift catches its staple diet of insects by flying quickly through the air with its large mouth open, each bird catching tens of thousands of insects each summer. The Swift is one of the latest of our summer migrants to arrive in Ireland and earliest to depart after breeding.

Ad.

Juv.

Ads.

Juv.

Sand Martin | Gamhlán gainimh | *Riparia riparia*
L 12cm   WS 28cm   Sp/Su/A   CB   Farmland/Wetland

A bit smaller than Robin; slim; sexes similar; rarely seen on ground; will perch on wires occasionally and reeds when roosting. **In flight**: dark brown upperparts; pale underside; dark brown breast band; plain dark wings; short, forked tail. Often sweeps the wings back and close to body in buoyant flight; does not glide much. **Juv/Im**: scaly upperparts; underside buffer; breast band faint/absent. Nests in burrows in sand cliffs, quarries, riverbanks; will occasionally use man-made holes in bridges/walls. **Voice:** include a short *brrtt*/a sharp *tcheerup*. Its song is a collection of weak, twittering notes. (See House Martin p. 181, young Swallow p. 182.)

nest

Juv.

Ad.

House Martin | Gabhlán binne | *Delichon urbicum*
L 12–14cm WS 28cm Sp/Su/A CB Farmland/Suburban

About the size of Robin; sexes similar; rarely seen on ground, usually only when collecting mud for nest building. Very short legs covered with white feathers. **In flight**: black with metallic-blue sheen; square white rump patch; short, forked tail. From below, white body/black wings. Juv: slightly duller plumage. Glides a lot; fluttering flight. Will perch on wires (very rarely on trees). Usually nests under eaves on outside of buildings and overhangs of other structures; will also use natural sites such as cliffs. **Voice**: loud, clear *prreet*, usually heard near the colony. (See Sand Martin p. 180, Swallow p. 182.)

Juv.

Ad.

Ad.

Ad.

chicks
on
nest

Juv.

Ad.

Ad

Swallow | Fáinleog | *Hirundo rustica*
L 17–22cm WS 32–34cm Sp/Su/A CB Farmland

About size of Starling; slim; small, straight beak; short, dark legs; usually nests on ledges inside buildings (barns/outhouses). Rarely seen on ground; regularly perches on wires (rarely in trees); roosts in reed beds before migration; sexes similar. **Adult**: red-brown face; long, deeply-forked tail (slightly longer on males); glossy blue-black upperparts; dark breast band; pale cream belly/undertail. **Juv/Im**: pale face/shorter forked tail. **In flight**: white spots across middle of tail (visible only when spread); dark upperparts; pale underside. Very agile/acrobatic flight. **Voice**: chatters a lot in flight/resting; makes loud, sharp calls when it sees predators. (See House Martin p. 181, Sand Martin p. 180.)

Swift | Gabhlán gaoithe | *Apus apus*
L 16–17cm   WS 42–48cm   Sp/Su/A   CB   Urban/Suburban/Farmland

Smaller/slimmer than Starling; sexes similar; tiny, dark beak; short, dark legs; rarely seen on ground; occasionally clings to walls. Nests inside cavities, usually under eaves of buildings. **Adult in flight**: all dark except for pale throat, visible only at close range; short, forked tail, looks pointed when closed; long, sickle-shaped wings; rapid wingbeats; often gather at dusk in large, noisy groups, high in the sky, sometimes heard but not seen. **Juv/Im in flight**: fine, pale barring on body. **Voice:** distinctive sound of summer is a group of Swifts, screaming with high-pitched, buzzing calls, speeding low over houses/streets.

Wagtails, Pipits, Larks and Dipper

Both wagtails and pipits are insect eaters and have a very horizontal posture. They spend most of their time on the ground but will readily take to a bush or tree. They all walk or run rather than hop on the ground. All have pale or white outer tail feathers.

As the name suggests, the wagtails are a group of insect-eating birds with long tails that they often wag up and down. Their plumage is usually quite vivid and their songs are fairly simple. They generally nest in a covered hollow, such as a crevice in the base of a tree overhanging a stream or river or on a ledge under a bridge.

Pipits are generally duller looking than the wagtails with brown-and-buff plumage with dark and light streaks, well suited for their preferred habitat of open grassy places. Their songs are usually relatively complicated and they often perform a song flight, which involves rising up into the air from the ground and gliding or dropping back down while singing.

Larks are famous singers and share the same plumage colours and habitats as the pipits. Many have crests and most have a very long

hind claw on the foot. They also perform song flights during the breeding season. Our skylark is well known for its ability to sing continuously while rising so high in the sky that it almost impossible to see. Unlike the pipits, they can have very elaborate songs that incorporate mimicry. They all nest on the ground.

Dippers are a group of birds found in Europe, North Africa, Asia and North and South America. They are all designed for hunting insects underwater and are the only true land bird to do so. They are never found far from fresh water. The Dipper gets its name from the way it hunts, 'dipping' underwater and walking along the bed of the river or stream searching for prey as it goes. Its legs and feet are very strong and anchor it while underwater. When it pops up again it will sometimes swim or float with wings half open or emerge onto a rock. It will also hunt for insects above, on or near water. The nest is large and a bit like that of a wren, built by both the male and female and is made mainly of moss. It is roughly spherical with an entrance hole on the side, angled towards the river. The nest cup is usually lined with fine plant material.

Pied Wagtail

NBr. F.

NBr. M.

'Whit Wagt

Br. M.

NBr. F.

NBr. M.

Juv.

Juv.

Pied Wagtail | Siubháinín an bhóthair | *Motacilla alba*
L 16–18cm WS 28cm AY CB Suburban/Urban/Farmland/Coast

About size of Robin; long, wagging tail; thin, black beak; long, dark legs. **Male**: upper-parts black, except for two white wing bars; white face; black forehead/throat; black bib; white belly/undertail coverts; flanks dark grey; long, black tail with white outer tail feathers, wagged frequently; throat white in winter. The continental race (known as White Wagtail; occurs in Sp/A) has pale grey back. **Female/Juv/Im**: dark grey mantle/back/upper wing coverts. **In flight**: black and white; undulating, short bursts of wingbeats followed by dipping glides with wings closed. Often runs away rather than flies. **Voice**: an explosive, high *tchizzik*. Song similar to call notes but longer/twittering.

Br. F.

Juv.

Br. F.

Br. F.

Ad.

Br. M.

Ad.

Br. F.

Grey Wagtail | Glasóg liath | *Motacilla cinerea*
L 18–20cm WS 25–26cm AY CB Wetland

About same size as Starling but slimmer; sharp, thin, dark beak; long, pale pink-brown legs. **Male**: breast/belly/undertail yellow; black chin/throat only in breeding plumage; grey head/mantle/back; thin, white supercilium; yellow rump; black tail with white outer feathers, as long as its body. **Female**: resembles male but has white throat/belly; yellow breast/undertail. **Juv/Im**: have a hint of brown in the grey; only yellow on undertail; pale on beak. **In flight**: noticeable white wing bar/white outer tail feathers; undulating flight. **Voice**: call is a loud *zeet-eet*, made when disturbed or in flight. (See Yellow Wagtail p. 192)

in parachute
song flight

Juv.

Ad. Br.

Ad. Br.
(worn)

Ad.
(autumn)

Juv.

Ad.
(spring)

Ad.

Meadow Pipit | Riabhóg mhóna | *Anthus pratensis*
L 14cm WS 24cm AY CB Farmland/Upland/Coast

Robin-sized ; slimmer; sexes similar; short, fine beak; pink legs. Resembles miniature thrush. **Adult**: dull brown head; fine dark streaking on crown; back streaked black/brown; long, thin tail; white outer tail feathers; pale buff throat; black streaking on breast/flanks/upper belly. Looks pale in summer/bright in autumn. **Juv/Im**: similar to adult; lacks dark streaks on flanks. **In flight**: slightly bouncy; white outer tail feathers visible as takes off. **Voice**: call high sharp *weeep*. Complex song: starting high-pitched/accelerating *seep* notes/ending with melodious trill. Usually sung while rising from ground/ends with bird dropping, its tail raised, like a parachute. (See Rock Pipit p. 189, Tree Pipit p. 192.)

Rock Pipit | Riabhóg chladaigh | *Anthus petrosus*
L 15–17cm WS 24cm AY CB Coast/Estuary

A bit bigger than a Robin; bigger than Meadow Pipit; sexes similar. **All ages**: like a duller, smoky version of its close relative the Meadow Pipit. Streaking on the back is almost absent; greyer below; outer tail feathers grey, *not white*; dark brown legs. Beak longer and stouter than Meadow Pipit, all dark in Br., pale base in NBr. **In flight**: undulating, dull and featureless with a long tail, grey outer tail feathers not very noticeable. **Voice**: call a thin *tweep*, thinner than Meadow Pipit. Song very similar to Meadow Pipit, though less musical. (See Meadow Pipit p. 188, and Tree Pipit p. 192.)

Skylark | Fuiseóg | *Alauda arvensis*
L 16–18cm WS 33cm AY CB Farmland

Robin-sized; pink legs; large hind claw; pale, stubby, pointed beak. **Adult**: crest on head, sometimes kept flat; long, slightly forked tail; white outer tail feathers; streaked light/dark brown upperparts; light buff breast/fine dark streaking; white belly. **Juv/Im**: brighter/more strongly marked; no crest. **In flight**: slightly forked tail; white outer tail feathers; thin, pale trailing edge to secondaries/inner primaries. If disturbed, usually flutters short distance, lands in long grass, then runs off. Undulating flight/wings completely closed on downward glide. **Voice**: song flight, see p. 184; folds wings near ground, drops into vegetation with almost continuous, energetic jumble of twittering, warbling sounds. Call a loud thin *chirrup*.

Dipper | Gabha dubh/Lon abhann | *Cinclus cinclus hibernicus*
L 18–20cm WS 28cm AY CB Wetland

Slightly smaller than a Blackbird; sexes similar; short, straight, black beak; fairly long, stout black legs. **Adult:** unmistakeable; all dark with brilliant white throat and breast; at close range the area just below the white breast is dark chestnut; short, stumpy tail; **Juv/Im:** greyer than adult; lacks white bib; pale grey underparts; scaly grey appearance. **In flight:** fast and straight, continuous rapid wingbeats. **Voice:** usually short, loud, harsh *tsit*.

Yellow Wagtail ('Blue-headed' Form)

Yellow Wagtail | Glasóg bhuí |
Motacilla flava
L 15–17cm   WS 23–27cm
A   RB   Farmland

Similar in size and appearance to Grey Wagtail, p. 187; can look very yellow overall. **All ages**: usually fairly broad, pale edges to all wing feathers, yellowish-green back, duller on Juv/Im; many races with large variation of the head pattern ranging from all black to pale brown and yellow. Never black or dark markings in the throat. Usually seen away from water but can be found on the coast during spring/autumn migration.

Yellow Wagtail

Tree Pipit | Riabhóg choille | *Anthus trivialis*
L 14–17cm   WS 25–27cm   A   NB   Farmland
Almost identical to Meadow Pipit, p. 188; white belly; best separated from Meadow Pipit by call, which is longer, thinner and slightly buzzing. A difficult bird to identify for the first time.

Note: Images not to scale

Thrushes

Blackbird

This is a fairly large group of related species and includes not only birds with the word 'thrush' in their name but also the Robin, chats, wheatears and redstarts. They are found in many parts of the world. Many are good singers.

The Robin and Blackbird are very familiar members of this group and need no introduction. Those with the word 'thrush' in their name tend to have spots and streaking on breast and belly. They have a very mixed diet ranging from fruit, especially berries, to insects and earthworms. In Ireland we have the Song and Mistle Thrush and these are joined in winter by Redwing and Fieldfares from Northern Europe.

The chats are small, upright-looking birds that usually hunt by pouncing on insect prey from an exposed perch, usually on a bush or low vegetation. We have two species in Ireland: the relatively common Stonechat and the scarce Whinchat.

Wheatears tend to hunt insects on the ground or from a low perch and almost all have boldly patterned black-and-white tails. The Wheatear, which is the only breeding wheatear found in Ireland, is a long-distance migrant and summer visitor from Africa. Wheatears that breed in Greenland and Arctic Canada pass through Ireland each year going to and coming back from Africa where they spend the winter. It is the only North American land bird to winter regularly this side of the Atlantic.

Redstarts are robin-like birds with red-orange tails. In Ireland they are usually seen on migration, especially in the autumn, a few overwinter and there is a very small breeding population.

Ad.

Juv.

Juv.
moultir
to Ad.

Ad.

Juv.

Ad.

Robin | Spideóg | *Erithacus rubecula*
L 13–14cm WS 21cm AY CB Farmland/Garden/Woodland

Adult: bright red-orange breast; grey forehead, side of the neck and upper breast; white belly; warm brown upperparts; stands upright; round appearance. **Juv/Im:** young birds, just out of the nest do not have a red breast, but instead are scaled light and dark brown; buff spots and streaks on the back and wings. **In flight:** flies fast and straight. **Voice:** call is a loud, thin *ptic*, usually repeated several times, often out of sight. It sings all year round but is at its loudest during spring, when its melodious twittering is often performed from a fence post or a prominent bush.

Female 'sunning'

Leucistic

Ad. F.

Ad. F.

Ad. M.

Ad. M.

1st W. F.

1st W. M.

Juv.

Juv.

Blackbird | Lon dubh | *Turdus merula*
L 24–26cm   WS 36cm   AY   CB   Woodland/Farmland/Garden

Male: jet-black; short, heavy, bright orange-yellow beak and eye ring; dark legs. Young males superficially resemble females. Partial or total albino birds sometimes seen. **Female**: dark chocolate-brown; paler streaked throat/breast (sometimes faintly spotted); no eye ring; usually duller beak. **Juv/Im**: dark beak; birds just fledged rich brown with pale streaks/spots. **In flight**: looks all dark; fast, straight flight. On landing will often droop its wings/cock its tail high in air. **Voice**: sings from a high, prominent position; melodious and loud, sometimes continuing for a long period. Calls include a loud *chock*/a high-pitched, thin *sseeee*. If disturbed, usually flies away making loud, excited calls. (See Ring Ouzel p. 203.)

Thrushes | 195

Song Thrush | Smólach | *Turdus philomelos*
L 21–23cm WS 34cm AY CB Woodland/Farmland/Garden

Slightly smaller/less robust than Blackbird. Small, sharp beak looks up-tilted; long,
pink legs. **All ages**: upperparts warm brown; pale buff breast; white belly with
conspicuous black V-shaped spots, forming lines, thinnest on throat/upper breast,
thickest with largest spots on flanks/belly. **In flight**: dark/unmarked upperparts; pale
buff-orange underwing coverts. On open ground often makes short dashes. **Voice**:
a loud *thick*, repeated several times quickly. The song, delivered from a high perch,
roof or satellite dish, is similar to that of Blackbird, but more musical/structured,
containing short phrases repeated clearly two to four times. (See Mistle Thrush
p. 197, Redwing p. 198.)

Mistle Thrush | Smólach mór | *Turdus viscivorus*
L 26–28cm WS 45cm AY CB Farmland/Suburban

Larger than Blackbird; on the ground it stands very erect and looks pot-bellied; dark beak with yellow base; long, pale legs. **All ages**: white underside with fine streaks and blotches on the throat and breast; belly has large distinct dark spots, not always forming lines. Dusty grey-brown upperparts; wing feathers are pale-fringed. **In flight**: white underwing; pale tip and edge to outer tail feathers; very undulating flight, glides with wings closed. **Voice**: call is a distinctive, rapid, harsh, chattering *tuck-tuck-tuck*, often heard in flight. Its song is similar but less musical and more repetitive than a Blackbird. (See Song Thrush p. 196.)

Redwing | Deargán sneachta | *Turdus iliacus*
L 20–22cm WS 34cm A/W/Sp NB Farmland/Garden

Smaller than Blackbird; sexes similar. **All ages**: rusty-red flanks, prominent pale supercilium, heavy streaking on throat, breast and flanks. **1st W.**: obvious white tips to some tertials and buff tips to some greater coverts. **In flight**: rusty-red underwing coverts and flanks, dark brown upperparts; flies straight; usually seen in flocks. **Voice**: call is a distinctive, high, wheezing *tzeeee*, regularly heard in flight and often heard from migrating birds passing overhead at night in late autumn and winter. (See Song Thrush p. 196.)

Fieldfare | Sacán | *Turdus pilaris*
L 23–27cm WS 40cm A/W/Sp NB Farmland/Garden

A bit bigger than Blackbird; sexes similar; straight, sharp, pale yellow, black-tipped beak; long, dark legs. **All ages**: grey head; large, grey rump patch and long, all-dark tail; pale yellow-brown throat and breast with dark streaking; large, black V-shaped spots on the flanks. **In flight**: all-dark tail; grey rump patch; white underwing coverts. Flight path straight. **Voice**: soft Blackbird-like notes and harsh, scratchy alarm calls.

M.

NBr. M.

NBr. M.

Juv. moulting

Br. M.

F.

Juv.

1st. W. F.

Juv.

Stonechat | Caislín dearg | *Saxicola rubicola*
L 12cm   WS 20cm   AY   CB   Upland/Farmland/Coast

Slightly smaller than Robin; dark beak/legs. **Male:** black head; white patches on the side of the neck/wings; bright orange breast/flanks; creamy-white rump; short, black tail; in NBr duller, paler plumage. **Female:** paler brown version of male; no white on rump/neck; less striking orange-brown breast. **Juv/Im:** a little like young Robin; brown with heavy streaking/spotting; red-brown rump. **In flight:** makes short flights to catch flies/pounces on insects on ground from a prominent position; straight, weak, buzzing flight. **Voice:** named after its loud call, a short *tchack-tchack* (like two stones being banged together), sometimes preceded by longer, thin *weeet*/accompanied by wing- and tail-flicking. (See Whinchat p. 203.)

Br. M.

Br. M.

Br. M.

Br. M.

Br. F.

Ad. F. (spring)

Ad. F./1st W.

Ad. F./1st W.

Juv.

Ad. F./1st W.

Wheatear | Clochrán | *Oenanthe oenanthe*
L 15cm WS 29cm Sp/Su/A CB Upland/Coast

Slightly bigger than Robin; often upright stance; dark, pointed beak; long, dark legs. **All ages**: white rump and tail with a broad, black, upside-down T-shaped tail band. **Male**: grey back, dark wings, dark face mask, upright posture on long legs. In autumn retains same pattern but becomes sandy brown with buff edges to the wing feathers. **Female**: similar to autumn male but lacks the dark face mask; plain, dark brown wings; grey-brown back. **Juv/Im**: similar to female. **In flight**: black-and-white tail and rump very noticeable. **Voice**: a weak squeak and also harsh *tjack*.

Ad. F. or Im.

Ad. F. or Im.

Ad. M.

Ad. F. or Im.

Ad. M.

Ad. F. or Im.

Ad. F. or Im.

Black Redstart | Earrdheargán dubh | *Phoenicurus ochruros*
L 14cm WS 24cm A/W/Sp NB Coast/Farmland

Size and shape of a Robin, regularly flicks its tail; dark, pointed beak; long, dark legs.
Male: sooty grey, darker on the face and breast; fiery red-orange tail with darker
central tail feathers; some white on inner wing; blacker on face and underside in Br
plumage. **Female/Juv/Im**: similar to male but grey-brown and no white on the wings.
In flight: fiery red-orange tail with darker central tail feathers and dark body. **Voice**:
call a high-pitched *zist* and also a *tick* sound. (See Common Redstart p. 203.)

Scarce & Rare

Whinchat | Caislín aitinn | *Saxicola rubetra*
L 12–14cm WS 21–24cm
Su/A SB Upland/Farmland

Similar to Stonechat, p. 200. **All ages**: unlike Stonechat, it has a broad, long, pale supercilium. In flight: no white on the rump: dark tail with white patches at the base. **Adult male**: supercilium bright white; head and back streaked.

M.

1st W./F.

Ring Ouzel | Lon creige | *Turdus torquatus*
L 23–26cm WS 38–42cm
Sp/S/A RB Upland/Coast on migration

Similar in size and shape to Blackbird, p. 195. **Male**: white breast patch and pale-edged grey wing feathers. **Female**: duller than male. **Juv/Im**: similar to female but pale breast patch almost invisible. Beware of leucistic Blackbirds (p. 195) which can have similar white patches.

M.

M.

Redstart | Earrdheargán | *Phoenicurus phoenicurus*
L 13–14cm WS 21–24cm
A RB Woodland/Farmland

Similar to Black Redstart, p. 202; female/juv/im and male in NBr plumage much paler and not grey looking, especially on the underside; male in Br plumage has black face, marmalade-orange breast and belly; white edge to front of crown.

M.

F.

Note: Images not to scale

Warblers, Crests, Flycatchers and Wrens

Warblers are a large group of small to medium-sized birds. Most are insect eaters though some will also eat fruit, especially outside the breeding season. Most are long-distance migrants and almost all in Ireland spend the winter in sub-Saharan Africa. In recent decades very small numbers of two species, the Blackcap and Chiffchaff, have spent the winter here. Warblers tend to be very good singers.

Crests are small, warbler-like birds that get their name from their bright crests. The Goldcrest is the smallest bird in Europe, weighing only about 6g and measuring just 9cm from the tip of its beak to the tip of its tail. They are insect eaters, often hovering while picking insects from leaves.

Flycatchers, as the name suggests, are insect eaters. They all catch insects by darting out from a perch on a bush or tree to grab a flying insect and returning to a perch to watch and wait for the next opportunity. All are long-distance migrants. Irish flycatchers

Goldcrest

spend the winter in sub-Saharan Africa.

Wrens are found in many parts of the world and here in Ireland we have one species. They all have stiff tails, which they often hold cocked high in the air. They are mainly insect eaters. The Latin name for our wren means 'cave-dweller', which aptly describes its behaviour as it spends most of its time deep inside hedges, bushes and undergrowth. Its ball-shaped nest has a hole on the side and during the breeding season usually contains five or six eggs, though up to 15 have been recorded. With an average life span of less than two years, it ensures its survival by providing many young. It is estimated that 5 million wrens breed in Ireland each year, nesting in hedges, stone walls, cliffs, bogs and even old teapots. It feeds mainly on insects and spiders which it hunts in dense undergrowth, usually venturing out into the open only to burst into song.

Juv.

Ad.
(spring)

Ad.
(autumn)

Chiffchaff | Tiuf-teaf | *Phylloscopus collybita*
L 10–11cm   WS 17–18cm   Sp/Su/A   CB   Woodland/Farmland/Garden

Roughly Wren-sized; sexes similar; difficult to distinguish from Willow Warbler (p. 207) apart from its song. **All ages:** upperparts green-grey; underside light yellow-grey; thin, dark eye stripe; narrow, dull supercilium; legs/beak usually dark grey-black**. In flight**: weak, slightly undulating flight; moves busily from branch to branch in search of insects; flicks wings/tail. **Voice**: unmistakeable song, a loud, high-pitched, strident, bouncing *chiff-chaff-chiff-chiff-chaff* lasting five or more seconds at a time. Its call is a soft *wheeet*. Usually heard in spring before Willow Warbler, with overwintering birds singing as early as beginning of March. (See Willow Warbler p. 207, Goldcrest p. 209.)

Juv.

Ad.

Ad.

Ad.

1st W.

Willow Warbler | Ceolaire sailí | *Phylloscopus trochilus*
L 11–12cm WS 18–19cm Sp/Su/A CB Woodland/Wetland

Slightly bigger than Wren. To all but very experienced birdwatchers looks identical to Chiffchaff; one of few birds here that is identified more easily by its song. **All ages**: similar in size/shape/pattern to Chiffchaff, but usually brighter/more yellow-looking; longer-winged appearance; legs usually pale. **Im**: brighter/yellower than adult. **In flight**: looks weak, slightly undulating; moves busily from branch to branch searching for insects, sometimes flicking wings/tail. **Voice**: song is a loud, clear, cascading warble, quiet/slow at start, louder/faster at end, lasting three or four seconds. Call is a soft short *wooeet*, similar to Chiffchaff. (See Chiffchaff p. 206; Goldcrest p. 209.)

Blackcap | Caipín dubh | *Sylvia atricapilla*
L 13–14cm WS 22cm Sp/Su/A/W CB Woodland/Garden

About the size of Robin. Can be very aggressive at a bird table. **Male**: neat jet-black cap; cold brown-grey body; pale throat, vent and undertail coverts. **Female/Juv/Im**: less noticeable, pale chestnut-brown cap, usually brighter on young birds; slightly browner overall. **In flight**: no noticeable markings on the body or wings. **Voice**: call is a harsh *tcek* repeated many times if alarmed. The song is a series of very varied, warbling notes, becoming louder towards the end. (See Garden Warbler p. 215)

crest flat

crest raised

M.

Juv.

Goldcrest | Dreoilín easpaig/ Dreoilín ceannbhuí | *Regulus regulus*
L 9cm   WS 14cm   AY   CB   Woodland/Farmland/Garden

Smallest bird in Europe; smaller than Wren; sexes similar. **Adult**: orange/yellow crown stripe on male/yellow on female, bordered in black at sides; large dark eye on plain face; short, dark line from base of beak giving a slightly sad expression; short, pale wing bar with rectangular black patch behind it. Sometimes raises/spreads out crown feathers. **Juv/Im**: lacks crown stripe. **In flight:** buzzing flight; hovers to pick insects from foliage. **Voice**: usually heard before bird is seen; a very thin, high-pitched call, erratic *szitt-szitt-szitt*. Song is high-pitched; includes rapid *fh-he-hee*, usually repeated four times, followed by similar, more varied phrase. (See Firecrest p. 216, Yellow-browed Warbler p. 216.)

Whitethroat | Gilphíb | *Sylvia communis*
L 14cm WS 20cm Sp/Su/A CB Woodland/Farmland/Coast

Size of a Robin; short beak, long tail; pale yellowish legs. **Male**: grey head, white throat, white eye ring, pink wash on breast and belly, rusty-brown on the wings, long, grey-brown tail with white outer tail feathers. **Female/Juv/Im**: brown instead of grey head and buff instead of pink on underside. **Voice:** harsh, chattering song sung from a bush or in flight. (See Lesser Whitethroat p. 215.)

Sedge Warbler | Ceolaire cíbe | *Acrocephalus schoenobaenus*
L 12–13cm   W 19cm   Sp/Su/A   CB   Wetland

About size of Robin; sexes similar; heard more often than seen. **Adult**: upperparts buff-brown back with dark streaks; dark wings; red-brown rump; short, dark, square-ended tail; pale buff supercilium, dark eye stripe/crown; underside cream with buff flanks. **Juv/Im**: fine dark streaks on side of breast. **In flight**: rarely seen flying beyond the reed bed it occupies for summer; usually just flutters short distance with tail dipped, sometimes while singing. **Voice**: long series of jumbled musical phrases, interspersed with a rattling *tchurr*; includes mimicked sounds of other birds. Usually sings near top of reed stem or bush. Its call is a short *tchok*. (See Reed Warbler p. 217, Grasshopper Warbler p. 212.)

Grasshopper Warbler | Ceolaire casarnaí | *Locustella naevia*
L 13cm WS 17cm Sp/Su CB Wetland/Young Conifer Plantation/Coast

About size of Dunnock; similarly dull plumage; thin, dark beak; pink legs; very secretive, often seen on or close to ground. **All ages**: dull yellow-brown upperparts; dark flecks on wings/back; white underside with pale tan wash/faint streaks on breast/flanks; relatively long, wedge-shaped tail, some spotting underneath. **Voice**: distinctive, consists of a sound like rapid, clicking noise of winding fishing reel. Its song is similar to some species of grasshopper, though not those found in Ireland. It usually sings from a prominent position such as top of a bush/post/branch. Once it finds a mate it does not sing as much. (See Sedge Warbler p. 211.)

Ad.

Ad.

Ad.

Ad.

Ad.

Ad.

Ad.

Juv.

Spotted Flycatcher | Cuilsealgaire | *Muscicapa striata*
L 14cm WS 24cm Sp/Su/A CB Woodland/Farmland

About size of Robin; drab looking; sexes similar; thin, short beak; dark legs. Name misleading as there is streaking, not spotting, on adults. Usually seen alone, sitting erect on exposed branch near bottom of a tree. **Adult:** closely streaked grey-white/dark-brown crown, peaked at rear; throat/breast/belly very pale grey-brown; dark streaks on breast/flanks; undertail coverts white; wings dark grey-brown, faint wing bar; back slightly paler. **Juv/Im:** cream tips to some upper wing coverts/back feathers. **In flight:** darts out from its perch with a broad, agile sweep to catch an insect in mid-air, returning to same position or nearby branch. **Voice:** low harsh *tsee* call; unremarkable song.

Ju

Ad.

Wren | Dreoilín | *Troglodytes troglodytes*
L 9–10cm WS 14–16cm All Year CB Woodland/Farmland/Garden

A tiny, rusty-brown bird; smaller than a Blue Tit; often cocks its tail so high it almost touches the back of its head. **All ages**: brown looking; pale supercilium; some dark bars and pale spots on short wings; fairly long, thin, downcurved beak; long, thin, yellow-brown legs. **In flight**: short, rounded wings; low, straight, buzzing flight. **Voice**: the song is very loud, high and energetic; cocks its tail when singing. It has a variety of calls, the most noticeable being a loud short *tchic*, often repeated many times in an irregular, mechanical fashion. (See Dunnock p. 240.)

Scarce & Rare

Wood Warbler | Ceolaire coille | *Phylloscopus sibilatrix*
L 11–12cm WS 19–24cm Su/A RB Woodland

Similar in size and appearance to Willow Warbler, p. 207; usually brighter lemon-yellow face and throat; white breast and belly; thin, dark eye stripe. **Voice:** distinctive song; high pitched and sounding like a spinning coin slowing down on a hard surface.

Garden Warbler | Ceolaire garraí | *Sylvia borin*
L 13–14cm WS 20–24cm
Su/A SB Woodland/near Wetland

Very similar in size and appearance to a Blackcap (p. 208) but lacks the black or chestnut cap and has a slightly thicker beak; no noticeable markings on the wing or body; grey on side of neck sometimes noticeable. **Voice:** call is a repeated short, slightly buzzing harsh chirping sound. Song short but like a speeded-up Blackbird.

Lesser Whitethroat | Gilphib bheag | *Sylvia curruca*
L 13–14cm WS 16–20cm A NB Farmland

Slightly smaller than Blackcap, p. 208; grey crown; darker ear coverts; white throat; grey-brown back and black legs; no noticeable body markings. Unlike Whitethroat (p. 210), no colour contrast between wing and back.

Note: Images not to scale

Scarce & Rare *(cont'd)*

Pied Flycatcher | Cuilire | *Ficedula hypoleuca*
L 12–13cm WS 21–24cm A NB Woodland/Garden

Robin sized. NBr: plain brown upperparts; cream-white underside; secondary coverts and tertials form white patch on the closed wing and wing stripe in flight; white on edge of tail not reaching the tip. Br Male: black and white with white wing patch.

Firecrest | Lasairchíor | *Regulus ignicapilla*
L 9–10cm WS 13–16cm A NB Farmland/Woodland

Similar in size and appearance to Goldcrest (p. 209) but has a bright white supercilium and thin, black eye stripe; brighter yellowish-green back.

Yellow-browed Warbler | Ceolaire buímhalach | *Phylloscopus inornatus*
L 9–10cm WS 14–18cm A NB Farmland/Coast/Woodland

Like a cross between a Goldcrest (p. 209) and a Chiffchaff (p. 206); long, broad, pale yellow supercilium, thin dark eye stripe; wing pattern similar to goldcrest but wing bars pale yellow; white belly, vent and undertail coverts.

Reed Warbler | Ceolaire giolcaí | *Acrocephalus scirpaceus*
L 12–14cm WS 17–21cm S/A SB Wetland

As the name suggests usually found in reed beds; plain, greyish-brown upperparts, darkest on the wing tips; rich brown rump; warm buff underparts with white throat; relatively long, stout beak. Voice: very like Sedge Warbler (p. 211). Continuous chirps and chatters, sometimes mimicking other birds.

Pied Flycatcher (F.)

Pied Flycatcher (Br. M.)

Firecrest

Yellow-browed Warbler

Reed Warbler

Reed Warbler

Note: Images not to scale

Tits and Treecreepers

Tits are one of the most familiar groups of birds in Ireland as most come into gardens and readily take food from bird tables and peanut feeders. Most are insect eaters during the breeding season and like to build their nests in cavities, such as holes in walls and trees, and nest boxes. Most are not migratory and rarely travel very far from where they were born.

Treecreepers are a group of small insect-eating birds that specialise in hunting insects on and under the bark of trees. They are so specialised that they have developed very stiff tails to give them extra support and as a result usually only climb up trees. Treecreepers in Ireland are not migratory and rarely travel far from where they were born.

Blue Tit

Blue Tit | Meantán gorm | *Cyanistes caeruleus*
L 11–12cm WS 18cm AY CB Woodland/Farmland/Garden

Smaller than Robin; sexes similar. **Adult:** pale blue cap surrounded by a white halo; white ear coverts; dark eye stripe; green-blue back; wings blue with faint white wing bar; tail also blue; nape dark blue; breast and belly yellow. **Juv/Im:** similar in pattern to adults but paler and more yellow in overall colour. **In flight:** pale blue upperparts, no white on the tail, weak, bouncing flight; rapid wingbeats. **Voice:** like most members of the tit family, very vocal and has various call notes. The most characteristic are a very high *pfit-pfit-che-ha-ah-ah* and a lower, scolding *churr*.

Ad. M.

Ad. F.

Ad. M.

Ad. M.

Ad. M.

Juv.

Great Tit | Meantán mór | *Parus major*
L 13–15cm   WS 24cm   AY   CB   Woodland/Farmland/Garden

Same size as Robin; largest of tit family. **Adult**: Glossy jet-black head; bright white cheeks. Breast/belly bright yellow; black line down the centre, which is usually broad on males/narrow, incomplete on females. Yellowish-green back; dark blue-green primaries; secondaries/tail feathers dark with varying degrees of pale blue edging; white under tail coverts. **Juv/Im**: look more faded/yellow. **In flight**: white wing bar; white cheeks; white outer tail feathers (most noticeable from below). **Voice**: has a richly varied repertoire of calls, including a blue-tit-like *tchurrr*/distinct phrases usually repeated two to four times, one sounding like *teacher, teacher*.

Ad.

Juv.

Coal Tit | Meantán dubh | *Periparus ater*
L 10–12cm   WS 19cm   AY   CB   Woodland/Farmland/Garden

Smaller than Robin; dull looking compared to the other tits; sexes similar; short, thin beak; long, grey legs. Comes readily to bird tables and has a mischievous jizz. **All ages**: long, white patch on the nape; black head and white ear coverts; upperparts dark grey-brown, two faint white wing bars; underside pale buff-grey. **In flight**: weak, bouncing flight, short bursts of rapid wingbeats. **Voice**: calls and song are varied but include a high, forced *fee-chew* repeated several times. Also a very high, goldcrest-like *su-ee-ou, zit-zit-zit, su-ee-ou.*

Ad.

Juv.

Long-tailed Tit | Meantán earrfhada | *Aegithalos caudatus*
L 14cm WS 18cm AY CB Woodland/Farmland/Garden

Smaller than Robin; black eyes and legs; tiny beak. **All ages**: outsized black-and-white tail, as long as its small pink, black-and-white body. Head grey-white with broad, black stripe above eye; dark face on Juv; back/wings black; pink patches at base of wings; pale edges to secondaries. Throat/breast dirty white, becoming grey-pink on belly/ undertail. **In flight**: reluctant to fly even short distances. Weak, slightly undulating flight. Usually seen in flocks ranging in size from three or four to over 20. **Voice**: flocks in winter can be quite noisy, making a variety of calls, including high-pitched, fast, thin *ssee-ssee-ssee* and shorter, lower *chrup*. Its song is similar to its calls.

Treecreeper | Snag | *Certhia familiaris*
L 13cm   WS 19cm   AY   CB   Woodland

Size of Robin; creeping movement with quick, short hops; hugs tree trunk or branches as it moves up the tree, usually in a spiral, rarely moves down along a tree. **All ages**: thin, curved beak; pale legs. Complex pattern of dark and light brown and buff upperparts; silver-white throat and breast fading to pale brownish-white on vent and undertail coverts; long, stiff, sharply pointed dark tail feathers. **In flight**: usually seen flying only short distances between trees; undulating flight. **Voice**: calls and song very high pitched, some long, slightly buzzing *seep* calls.

Bearded Tit | Meantán croiméalach | *Panurus biarmicus*
L 13–15cm WS 16–18cm W RB/NB Wetland
Slightly bigger than a Long-tailed Tit, p. 223. likes reed beds. **Male**: very long tail; sandy-brown body with some black and white on the wings; pale blue-grey head; short, pale orange-yellow beak. **Female**: sandy-brown head. **Juv/Im**: sandy-brown head and black back.

Note: Images not to scale

Crows, Starlings and Waxwing

Seven members of the crow family are regularly found in Ireland, are represented in almost every habitat, and are probably the bird group most familiar to people here. Most have black plumage, some with white or grey also, and one, the Jay, has very colourful plumage. Some are scavengers and opportunistic hunters and will eat a wide range of food, from insects and seeds to carrion and human food waste. Others are more specialised, such as the Jay's likeness for acorns and Chough's preference for coastal grasslands. Their calls are fairly simple and unmusical. Most nest on their own in trees, on cliffs or old buildings; the Jackdaw nests in hollows in trees but also in loose colonies in chimney pots while the Rook nests in colonies in tall trees. All our crows are non-migratory and rarely travel far from where they were born.

Starlings are medium-sized birds with species found in Europe, Africa, Asia and Australia. They have also been introduced to North America and other countries. They can be very colourful and usually have glossy plumage. They generally hunt for insects on the ground but will also eat berries and other fruit. They are usually

Jay

found in flocks outside the breeding season and during the winter our Starlings are frequently joined by birds from Europe and will sometimes roost in huge flocks in reed beds or in woodland with numbers in excess of 100,000 individuals. The (Eurasian) Starling, our only common starling, is a great mimic and will incorporate the sounds of other birds and even artificial sounds like car alarms and whistles. It likes to nest in cavities and regularly exploits holes in the eaves of houses and can become a noisy and unwelcome lodger.

Waxwings are an unusual-looking group of birds. If you look closely at their wings, some of the feather tips look like they have been dipped in red wax, hence the name. In Europe they breed in northern forests. They are mainly fruit eaters with a fondness for berries. Because of this link with berries, in years when berry crops are poor, thousands migrate across Europe and sometimes reach Ireland in what is known as an invasion. During these invasion years they can turn up on their own or in flocks up on a berry bush almost anywhere in the country. At times they can appear to be very tame and approachable.

Jackdaw | Cág | *Corvus monedula*
L 32–34cm WS 68–72cm AY CB Suburban/Urban/Farmland

Smaller than Rook; a very neat-looking crow. **All ages**: silver-grey nape and side of neck; rest of the head black; pale blue iris; body a duller silver-grey; wings and fairly short tail black; fairly short stout, straight, black beak; legs black. **In flight**: short primary 'fingers'; more pointed than Rook; fairly stiff, quick wingbeats; flocks glide, twist and turn. **Voice**: higher pitched than Rook, includes harsh *keyaak* and *kew-kaw* sometimes repeated several times. (See Rook p. 229, Chough p. 232.)

Ad.

Ad.

Ad.

Juv.

Rook | Préachán/Rúcach | *Corvus frugilegus*
L 43–47cm WS 88–92cm AY CB Farmland/Suburban/Urban

Slightly bigger than Jackdaw. Black plumage with purple-blue sheen, duller and browner when worn; long, conical, slightly downcurved beak; black legs. **Adult:** outer half of beak dark; inner half/bare throat patch powdery-white; untidy feathers around thighs ('shaggy trousers'). Moves more slowly/deliberately on ground, 'gallops' away if approached. **Juv/Im:** 1ˢᵗ Y has all-black beak; black feathers on inner half of upper mandible. **In flight:** all dark; primaries clearly seen as 'fingers' at end of wings, not so noticeable on Jackdaw. **Voice:** typical *kaw*, can be repeated several times; often fans tail/stretches forward when calling. (See Jackdaw p. 228, Chough p. 232, Raven p. 230, Carrion Crow p. 236.)

Raven | Fiach Dubh | *Corvus corax*
L 62–66cm   WS 125–135cm   AY   CB   Upland/Farmland/Coast

Largest Irish crow. One and a half times the size of the Rook and twice the size of the Jackdaw. **All ages**: all-black plumage; massive beak, feathers extending out along the upper mandible. **In flight**: shows very obvious primary 'fingers'; tail wedge-ended, not round or square-ended like the Rook, Jackdaw or Chough. **Voice**: characteristic call, given either in flight or from a perch, when it often bobs its head up and down. It is a deep *ooooaawk* usually repeated several times. (See young Rook p. 229, Jackdaw p. 228, Chough p. 232, Carrion Crow p. 236.)

dropping shellfish

unusual pale wings

Ad.

Ad.

Juv.

Hooded Crow | Feannóg | *Corvus cornix*
L 47cm WS 87–99cm AY CB Farmland/Estuary/Coast

About the same size as a Rook; strong, straight, black beak; dark legs. **Adult:** black hood covering head, neck and breast, where it forms a rough-edged bib; rest of the body pale grey-brown; wings and tail black. **Juv/Im:** similar to adult but brown wash to the back and head feathers and less distinct bib. **In flight:** obvious pale back and belly. Some individuals can have unusual, broad, pale wing stripes. **Voice:** call is usually a loud hoarse *krraaa-krraaa-krraaa*. Some Hooded Crows spend a lot of time hunting on the seashore.

Chough | Cág cosdearg | *Pyrrhocorax pyrrhocorax*
L 38–40cm WS 70–82cm AY SB Coast

Slightly smaller than a Rook; sexes similar. **Adult**: curved red beak and long, pink-red legs, all-dark glossy black plumage. **Juv/Im**: pale orange-red beak. **In flight**: curved red beak, pink-red feet usually visible; all-dark plumage; outer primaries spread finger-like; short, slightly round-tipped tail. Often bouncing flight, sometimes dropping with folded wings and rising quickly up again. **Voice**: loud, high-pitched squeaky *cheeow* call. (See Rook p. 229, Jackdaw p. 228.)

growing tail

Magpie | Snag breac | *Pica pica*
L 42–50cm WS 56cm AY CB Farmland/Garden/Urban/Suburban

About size of Rook; sexes similar; legs/beak black. **Adult**: glossy black-and-white body/wings with long wedge-ended tail; blue-green sheen on the back/tail feathers. Will walk or hop on the ground, sometimes with tail raised. Can look tailless during moult or if after escaping an attack by a predator, such as a cat. **Juv/Im**: shorter tails and some white around the eye. **In flight**: long tail; black-and-white primaries; white 'braces' on the back. **Voice**: call is a harsh, mechanical *chakk-kackk-kackk*. Song is more musical with high squeaks. Noisy when alarmed, e.g. nearby cat or bird of prey.

Jay | Scréachóg choille | *Garrulus glandarius*
L 32–34cm   WS 54–56cm   AY   CB   Woodland/Garden

Same size as a Jackdaw; sexes similar. **All ages**: blue-and-black wing patch at the 'elbow'; white patch on the secondaries; large, white rump patch; long, black tail; pink-tinged, grey-brown body with white throat and undertail; black moustache; short, dark beak. **In flight**: white rump and blue patches on the wings; weak-looking, slow, fluttering flight. **Voice**: can be quite noisy, especially if alarmed, a loud, harsh screeching sound.

large winter flock

Ad. Br.

Ad. Br. F.

Ad. W.

Ad. Br. M.

Juv.

Juv. moulting
to 1st W.

Starling | Druid | *Sturnus vulgaris*
L 20–22cm WS 40cm AY CB Farmland/Suburban/Urban/Wetland

Blackbird-sized; long, pink legs. **Br:** glossy black with blue-green sheen; faint
spotting on back/undertail; pointed, yellow beak, base pale blue-grey (male)/pink
(female), short tail. **NBr:** dark glossy; heavily spotted, most concentrated on head;
pale brown-edged wing feathers, dark beak. **Juv/Im:** initially plain grey-brown, pale
throat, moulting to adult-like, pale-spotted, dark plumage. Head usually last to lose
plain grey-brown plumage. **In flight:** looks all dark; short tail; broad-based, short,
pointed wings. Straight or slightly bouncing flight with rapid wingbeats, gathers in
flocks, sometimes very big, before going to roost. **Voice:** calls/song very varied;
expert mimic including man-made sounds. (See Rose-coloured Starling p. 236.)

Scarce & Rare

Carrion Crow | Caróg dhubh | *Corvus corone*
L 45–47cm WS 85–100cm AY NB Farmland

Very similar in size and shape to Hooded Crow (p. 231) but all black. Smaller than Raven (p. 230) and has almost square-ended tail and a slimmer beak. Can be confused with young Rook (p. 229) which has a very pointed, dagger-shaped beak. Voice: similar to Hooded Crow. (See Rook p. 229, Raven p. 230.)

Ad.

Rose-coloured Starling |
Druid rósach | *Pastor roseus*
L 19–21cm WS 37–40cm
Sp/A NB Farmland/Garden

Same size and shape as Starling, p. 235. **Adult:** pale pink breast, belly, back and rump, duller in NBr. plumage. **Juv/Im:** pale yellow beak, dark towards the tip; paler body contrasting more with dark wings; neat pale edged wing feathers.

Juv.

Waxwing | Síodeiteach | *Bombycilla garrulus*
L 18–20cm WS 32–35cm W NB Farmland/Garden

Starling-sized and exotic looking; looks pinkish grey; prominent, rough head crest; black face; broad, bright yellow terminal tail band; yellow-and-white primary tips and waxy red tips to secondaries. Similar shape and flight action to Starling, usually seen in flocks on berry bushes. **Voice:** a high-pitched, metallic trill.

Note: Images not to scale

Sparrows, Dunnock, Finches and Buntings

Sparrows have strong, conical beaks, which they use for eating seeds, but they also eat insects, especially during the breeding season. Their plumage is not very bright and their songs and calls are not very musical. They are often associated with human activity, particularly farming, and because our sparrows like to nest in crevices and hollows they will sometimes nest in the eaves of

Tree Sparrow

buildings, even in urban areas. When not in a hollow, their nests are often covered with a dome. They are usually not migratory in Ireland. The House Sparrow has spread around the world with humans. In North America there are many birds with the name 'sparrow' that are not related to our sparrows.

The Dunnock is the odd one out in this section as it is mainly an insect eater with a fine, thin beak. It is included because visually it can be mistaken for one of the sparrows because of its dull brown plumage. In fact, it is so close in general appearance that it is sometimes called Hedge Sparrow. It is a member of the Accentor family, found across Europe and Asia, the other members of which are found at high altitudes. The name Dunnock comes from Old English, meaning 'little brown one'. Birdwatchers today often refer to birds like the dunnock as an 'LBJ' or 'Little Brown Job'.

Finches are small birds with conical beaks. They are more delicate than the sparrows, which they superficially resemble, but have more musical songs. They eat mainly seed but will also eat insects in the breeding season. Many are migratory and each winter finches in Ireland, such as the Chaffinch and Siskin, are joined by others from Europe. Unlike the sparrows they usually build open, cup-shaped nests in bushes and trees.

Buntings have conical beaks like the finches and sparrows though not as stout. Not as musical as the finches but their short songs can be very distinctive. They are often associated with farmland but are also found in bogs and reed beds as well as on the coast, especially in winter. They are usually seed eaters, with a particular preference for grass seeds, but will also eat insects, especially during the breeding season.

House Sparrow | Gealbhán binne | *Passer domesticus*
14–16cm   WS 24cm   AY   CB   Farmland/Suburban

Robin-sized; stubby, dark-grey, conical beak, paler on female/young; red-brown
legs. **Male**: black bib (reduced in NBr plumage); grey crown; dark brown eye
stripe extends/widens down nape; ear coverts/side of throat pale grey; breast/
belly dark-grey; tail long, dark brown with buff edges; grey rump; back streaked
light brown; wings light and dark brown; white wing bar. **Female**: unremarkable
plumage, paler, lacking black/white/richer browns of male. **In flight**: fast/straight,
undulates on longer flights. **Voice**: loud *cheep* repeated without variation. Often
heard calling/chattering in groups from bushes/hedges; dull colour makes it
almost invisible. (See Tree Sparrow p. 239, female Chaffinch p. 242.)

Tree Sparrow | Gealbhan crainn | *Passer montanus*
L 14cm   WS 24cm   AY   SB   Farmland

Slightly smaller than House Sparrow; sexes similar; grey conical beak, red-brown legs.
Adult: smooth chestnut-brown crown and nape; white cheek with dark spot; white
collar; very short black bib; grey-white breast and belly; back and wings a mixture of
light and dark brown and black; white wing bars. **Juv/Im**: faint pale collar; cheek grey
with indistinct dark spot; some grey on the crown. **In flight**: brown upperparts with
two short, thin, white wing bars. **Voice**: similar to House Sparrow; chirpy, chattering
call and song. (See male House Sparrow p. 238.)

recently
fledged
Juv

moulting

Dunnock | Bráthair an dreoilín | *Prunella modularis*
L 13–14cm   WS 20cm   AY   CB   Woodland/Farmland/Garden

Robin-sized; is not a sparrow; sexes similar; short, thin, black beak; long, thin, dark brown legs. When feeding hops along open ground, usually under bushes, comes to bird tables. **Adult**: upperparts dark brown, streaked black; dark grey neck and side of face; underside dark grey, paler toward undertail coverts; dark streaking on flanks; deep red or brown eye. **Juv/Im**: more heavily streaked than adult. **In flight**: dull brown; no noticeable features; slightly undulating but not very fast. **Voice**: call is a high thin *seeep*. The song is wren-like though not as loud or as long as wren's. (See Wren p. 214)

Ad.

Ad.

Ad.

Ad.

moulting Juv.

Juv.

feeding flock

Goldfinch | Lasair choille | *Carduelis carduelis*
L 12–13cm WS 24cm AY CB Woodland/Farmland/Garden

Roughly Robin-sized. **Adult**: blood-red face, white-and-black head; broad, bright yellow wing bars; rest of wings black, with white tips to the primaries and secondaries; tail black and white; pale golden brown back; paler rump. **Juv/Im**: birds just out of the nest are similar to the adults except that the head is completely pale brown. **In flight**: striking yellow-and-black wing pattern; undulating flight; rarely seen alone. **Voice**: long, beautiful song contains buzzes, characteristic fluid notes, trills and twitters. Calls almost continuously in flight. The call is simpler than the song and contains more fluid notes.

F.

M.

F.

Br. M

F.

NBr. M

F.

Br. M.

F.

NBr. M

Chaffinch | Rí rua | *Fringilla coelebs*
L 14–16cm WS 26cm AY CB Woodland/Farmland/Garden

Robin-sized. **Male**: face/breast/belly rosy orange-pink; crown/nape metallic blue-grey; brown back; rump olive-green. Wings dark brown with two white wing bars; white outer tail feathers on long dark tail. Adult/1st Y males are duller in NBr plumage, though not as dull as female. **Female**: same pattern as male but drab, pale grey-brown. **In flight**: double white wing bars/white outer tail feathers very obvious; white underwing. **Voice**: calls include a loud *buzz-twink-twink-twink*/in flight a low, weak *weiou*. Its song lasts about three seconds, is repeated, starts with buzzing notes, slows, descends into a jumble and finally a flourish. (See female House Sparrow p. 238, Brambling p. 243, Hawfinch p. 252.)

NBr. M.

NBr. F.

NBr. F.

NBr. F.

NBr. F.

NBr. M.

NBr. M.

NBr. M.

NBr. F.

Brambling | Breacán | *Fringilla montifringilla*
L 14–16cm   WS 26cm   W NB   Farmland

Similar size and shape to Chaffinch. **Male**: white rump patch, marmalade breast and wing patches. Dark scaly head and back in NBr plumage, becoming all dark in Br plumage. **Female**: similar to the male but duller looking. **In flight**: white rump patch, marmalade-orange on inner part of wings; dark tail with no obvious white outer tail feathers; usually seen in flocks in winter. **Voice**: high-pitched *tweeep* and repeated *chick* sound. (See Chaffinch p. 242.)

Bullfinch | Corcàn coille | *Pyrrhula pyrrhula*
L 15–17cm   WS 26cm   AY   CB   Farmland/Garden

A large, plump finch; slightly bigger than a Robin; short, heavy, dark grey conical beak. **Male**: jet-black crown and nape; throat, breast and belly vivid deep pink; large white rump patch; black tail; light grey back; black wings with a broad white wing bar. **Female**: vivid pink replaced by dull pale grey-brown; back also grey-brown; grey nape. **Juv/Im**: like female but lacks black cap. **In flight**: always showing bright white rump and all-dark tail, black cap, short, white wing bars, bouncing flight. **Voice**: the call is a weak, soft *weep*; song is a soft whistling chatter.

Crossbill | Crosghob | *Loxia curvirostra*
L 15–17cm WS 29cm AY SB Woodland/Upland

A bit bigger than Robin. **Male:** stout beak with crossed-over tips; pinkish-red body; dark wings and forked tail. **Female:** like male but green-grey body, bright yellow-green rump. **Juv/Im:** heavily streaked. **In flight:** often seen in flocks, stocky head, dull looking with no obvious markings, undulating flight. **Voice:** loud high-pitched *Schip-schip-schip* call. (See female/Juv Greenfinch p. 246)

NBr. M.

Br. M.

NBr. M.

F.

M. Br.

Juv.

F.

NBr. M.

Greenfinch | Glasán darach | *Chloris chloris*
L 15cm WS 26cm   AY   CB   Woodland/Farmland/Garden

Roughly Robin-sized; strong, conical, pinkish-grey beak; pink legs. **Male**: yellow-green body; bright yellow patches on the wings and base of the outer tail feathers; grey on wings and ear coverts. **Female**: drab, paler yellow patches. Both have a dark shadow around the eye. **Juv/Im**: streaked below and may resemble female Chaffinches, p. 242. **In flight**: flashes yellow and green; undulating flight. **Voice**: calls include a squeaky *whou-ie-ouh*, and buzzing notes. Will sometimes sing during a display flight, with stiff, mechanical wingbeats. Parts of its long, melodious, twittering song are often likened to that of a Canary. (See Female/Juv Crossbill p. 245)

Siskin | Píobaire | *Carduelis spinus*
L 11–12cm   WS 21–22cm   AY   CB   Woodland/Farmland/Garden

Smaller than Robin; pale, dark-tipped, pointed beak; reddish-brown legs. **Male**: black cap/throat; head dark olive-green, pale yellow stripe extending from eye back to nape down around ear coverts; wings black with two bright yellow wing bars; pale edges to secondaries; faintly dark-streaked, olive-green back; yellow rump, notched tail with yellow patches at base of outer feathers; green-yellow breast/upper belly; lower belly/undertail coverts white with dark streaking. **Female**: no black cap or chin; less yellow; heavily streaked back. **Juv/Im**: paler/more streaked than female. **In flight**: yellow/black; fast; undulating. **Voice**: include a variable twitter, very thin *tee-oou*, buzzing *wheeze* and a high, bouncing, chattering trill. (See Serin p. 252.)

Redpoll | Deargéadan | *Carduelis flammea*
L 12–13cm W 21–22cm AY CB Farmland/Garden

Slightly smaller/slimmer than Robin. **Male:** blood-red forehead; black bib; back dark brown with lighter streaks; wings darker with two pale buff wing bars (inner one is very faint); rump pale with faint dark streaks; tail short/slightly notched; breast deep pink in breeding season, buff in NBr plumage; white belly/vent/undertail coverts; flanks heavily streaked light/dark brown; short, stubby, pale yellow beak with dark culmen; short, black legs. **Female/Juv/Im:** blood-red forehead, duller, more streaked plumage. **In flight:** pale wing bars, very bouncy flight. **Voice:** includes high, thin, rising *oiu-eeee*, short, fast reeling notes and a *chi-chi-chi-chaa*. (See Linnet p. 249, Twite p. 252.)

Br. M.

Br. M.

NBr. M.

F.

F./1st W.

Br. M.

NBr. M.

Br. M.

moulting Juv.

F./1st W.

Linnet | Gleoiseoch | *Carduelis cannabina*
L 13–14cm WS 24cm AY CB Farmland

Size of Robin but slimmer; short, triangular grey beak; dark legs. **Male:** Br: bright red forehead/breast patches; rest of head grey; white belly; back rich brown; wings darker brown, bright white edges to primaries; tail notched/edged white. Duller in NBr plumage, losing bright red feathers. **Female/Juv/Im:** browner, streaked, no red or grey. **In flight:** noticeable diffuse pale flashes on wings, calls constantly, bouncing flight. **Voice:** flight call squeaky, like a wet cork rubbed against glass. Its song often a very long series of chirps, twitters, chatters and musical warbling notes. Often sings from the top of a bush/tree. (See Redpoll p. 248, Twite p. 252.)

F.

F.

F.

NBr. M.

Br. M.

Br. M.

NBr. M.

Yellowhammer | Buíóg | *Emberiza citrinella*
L 16cm WS 26cm AY CB Farmland

Slightly bigger than Robin. **Br**: male has bright yellow head, female duller; back/wings/tail a complex mixture of light/dark browns; rump bright red-brown; yellow throat/breast, streaked on female. **NBr**: dull looking; males/females similar; heavy grey-brown streaking on head/throat/breast/flanks, with yellow tinges to head/throat/lower belly. **In flight**: rusty rump; white outer tail feathers; looks long/slim. **Voice:** its distinctive song often first locates this bird in spring/summer; a loud clear wheezing song, with notes spaced as if saying rather quickly *little-bit-of-bread-and-no-cheeeeese*. Its call is a short, rough *schep*. (See female Reed Bunting p. 251, Corn Bunting p. 252, Lapland Bunting p. 252.)

. M.

**Br. M.
(moulting)**

Br. F.

**M.
(moulting)**

M.

NBr. M.

Br. M.

F.

Br. M.

F.

Reed Bunting | Gealóg ghiolcaí | *Emberiza schoeniclus*
L 14–16cm WS 24cm AY CB Wetland/Farmland

Robin-sized. **Male Br:** black head; white neck collar/moustache; black bib; back heavily streaked dark brown/buff; rump grey; wings have rich brown tones, no white; tail long, black with white outer feathers; underside pale grey; black streaks on flanks. **NBr:** male resembles female, plumage paler; faint black bib. **Female/Juv/Im:** less striking; dark brown head, white throat/moustache; faint white supercilium; no white neck collar. **In flight:** chestnut on wings; white outer tail feathers; undulating flight, rarely flies far. **Voice:** high, thin, descending *tzeeeu*. Song is a high, hesitant, buzzing variation on *weeet-weet-chit*, reminiscent of *'plink-plink-fizz'* and a lower, faster *chi-choo*. (See female Yellowhammer p. 250, Lapland Bunting p. 252.).

Scarce & Rare

Twite | Gleoiseach sléibhe | *Carduelis flavirostris*
L 13–14cm WS 22–24cm AY RB Farmland

Similar to Linnet (p. 249) and Redpoll (p. 248); differs in all plumages from both by plain pink/purple rump. **NBr**: separate from Linnet by yellow beak with dark tip; from Redpoll by lack of red on the forehead and browner looking.

Corn Bunting | Gealóg bhuachair | *Emberiza calandra*
L 17–19cm WS 26–32cm A NB Farmland

Slightly bigger than a Yellowhammer, p. 250; very stocky looking; drab brown with no obvious plumage markings; heavy, pale, conical beak; pale underside with dark streaking on breast and flanks; no white on tail. **Voice:** song a metallic jangling rising towards the end; a bit like a Yellowhammer but shorter and faster. Has recently become extinct as Irish breeding species.

Snow Bunting | Gealóg shneachta | *Plectrophenax nivalis*
L 16–18cm WS 32–38cm A/W NB Coast/Upland

Size of a Chaffinch, p. 242. **Br male**: black and white. **Female/NBr male**: white wings with large black wing tips; white tail with dark centre; pale beak dark tip; some brown on the head and back. **Juv/Im**: darker above, less white on the wing.

Lapland Bunting | Gealóg Laplannach | *Calcarius lapponicus*
L 14–16cm WS 26–28cm A/W NB Coast

Similar to female Reed Bunting, p. 251; chestnut-brown on nape; brown face with black edge to ear coverts; white-bordered chestnut panel on the wing. Likes open ground.

Hawfinch | Glasán gobhmór | *Coccothraustes coccothraustes*
L 17–18cm WS 29–33cm A/W NB Woodland

Size of a Bullfinch, p. 244; huge, conical, dark grey beak; pale brown head; pale iris; white tip to brown tail; broad white wing strip on primaries.

Serin | Seirín | *Serinus serinus*
L 11–12cm WS 20–23cm A NB Farmland

Similar to Siskin (p. 247) though looks larger headed and beak is grey, short and stubby; different at all ages with almost all-dark wings and tail and yellow rump. Male has yellow on head and breast but no black.